Other books by Gwendolyn MacEwen

poetry
Selah 1961
The Drunken Clock 1961
The Rising Fire 1963
Terror and Erebus 1965
A Breakfast for Barbarians 1966
The Shadow Maker 1969
The Armies of the Moon 1972
Magic Animals 1975
The Fire-Eaters 1976
The T.E. Lawrence Poems 1982
Afterworlds 1987

novels
Julian the Magician 1963
King of Egypt, King of Dreams 1971

short stories
Noman 1972
Noman's Land 1985

MERMAIDS AND IKONS
A Greek Summer

Gwendolyn MacEwen

First published in 1978 by House of Anansi Press Inc.
This edition published in Canada in 2017 and the USA in 2017
by House of Anansi Press Inc.
www.houseofanansi.com

House of Anansi Press is committed to protecting our natural environment.
As part of our efforts, the interior of this book is printed on paper that contains
100% post-consumer recycled fibres, is acid-free, and is processed chlorine-free.

21 20 19 18 17   1 2 3 4 5

Library and Archives Canada Cataloguing in Publication

MacEwen, Gwendolyn, 1941–1987, author
Mermaids and ikons : a Greek summer / Gwendolyn MacEwen.

Issued in print and electronic formats.
ISBN 978-1-4870-0263-3 (softcover).—ISBN 978-1-4870-0264-0 (EPUB).—
ISBN 978-1-4870-0265-7 (Kindle)

1. MacEwen, Gwendolyn, 1941–1987—Travel—Greece. 2. Greece—
Description and travel. 3. Greece—Social life and customs—20th century.
I. Title.

DF727.M33 2017   914.9504'7   C2017-901312-2
C2017-901313-0

Library of Congress Control Number: 2017933806

Series design: Brian Morgan
Cover illustration: Aaron Manczyk

*We acknowledge for their financial support of our publishing program
the Canada Council for the Arts, the Ontario Arts Council, and the
Government of Canada through the Canada Book Fund.*

Printed and bound in Canada

Mermaids and Ikons

INTRODUCTION
by Rosemary Sullivan

PART TRAVELOGUE, part narrative, part diary, *Mermaids and Ikons* offers a portrait of a poet's imagination at work. Unlike most travelogues, it is not a guide to *what* to see, but rather *how* to see. It is a map that invites you into the mind of the remarkable Canadian poet Gwendolyn MacEwen.

MacEwen was an autodidact. Whatever fascinated her had to be investigated thoroughly. Drawn to Middle Eastern cultures, she studied Hebrew in order to read Jewish esoteric texts and visited Israel when she was twenty-one, writing a novel set during the Arab–Israeli war of 1948. Later, she learned Arabic, visited Egypt, and wrote her remarkable novel *King of Egypt, King of Dreams,* about the monotheistic heretic, the *Pharaoh Akhenaten.* Finally, she learned Greek. According to Greek friends in Toronto, she spoke the language fluently and elegantly, indeed better than the man with whom she had fallen in love and who was her motive for learning it.

In the summer of 1971, Gwendolyn MacEwen and the Greek musician Nikos Tsingos travelled to Greece to get married. It was during the three months they spent there that MacEwen wrote the notes for her travelogue, only completing the book on a return trip to Greece with Tsingos in 1976.

As soon as she arrived in Greece, its astonishing light, its green translucent sea, and its exquisite landscapes consumed her. But she was not a tourist; she was an initiate into its complex mysteries, already deeply familiar with its art and history. She saw Greece as the place where East meets West, where light and dark conflict; she saw it as a cartography of the human psyche.

MacEwen must be the only traveller to Greece to begin an account of a trip to the Acropolis with a knitting party of women sitting in an Athenian kitchen, wielding their weapons of domesticity (she inadequately), while the Acropolis and its temples hover in the high wind beyond the window. She asks, "What is history when you live in it, when you are not time's tourists?" MacEwen loved what she felt was the Greeks' fervent and ferocious involvement in the present moment, so different from the Western tradition of self-control and the repression of emotion. It was evident in their language, with its impossible declensions and accompanying gesticulations, and in their passionate and possessive devotion to family. But such exuberance overlaid a dark and terrifying history, which even in modern times, let alone historically, included the brutal occupation by German fascists in World War II, the Civil War that began in 1946 and lasted three years, and the military dictatorship (1967 to 1974) that was in full swing when MacEwen visited.

In the pounding rain, MacEwen and Tsingos visited the ruins of the Byzantine fortress complex of Mystras, where she felt "soaked to the soul," "the rain of war falling," the "mud-slide" of History. She even had a vision of the great Byzantine emperor Constantine being crowned at Mystras in 1449. He looked like a little playing-card king set against all the sieges, the assassinations, and the slaughters of empire building. This is the dark shadow side of Greece. But then they visit Olympia, a world of pure sunlight, golden and seductive, with its temple of Zeus and its archaeological museum, in which they view Praxiteles' great statue of Hermes, so exquisite, with muscles, sinews, and veins almost visible beneath the skin, that it seems to exist in another dimension of reality. For MacEwen, the statue is an embodiment of "the purest form of man rejoicing in itself." These, then — the dark and the light — are the extremes of the human psyche.

For MacEwen, the past was not the past but human and utterly familiar. What is two thousand years in evolutionary time? To demonstrate, she translates the inscription on the sarcophagus of a Greek grandmother and child in the ancient necropolis of Kerameikos in Athens: "When I lived we beheld the light, now I hold her dead, being dead myself."

She and Tsingos travelled to the island of Paros, beloved by the great poet George Seferis — the island whose "streets and squares aspired to the condition of music," as he put it — and to its sister island, Antiparos, where Tsingos was born. It was almost déjà vu for MacEwen, as if she had been there before, and its message was simple. "You let it all hang out — birth, death, everything. If necessary, you overplay emotions; you do not understate, you do not conceal. It is the only way." And everything demands *attention*!

Why does she call her travelogue *Mermaids and Ikons*? They are the polarities of her imaginative universe. Mermaids are not those safe little creatures in Hans Christian Andersen's story, but instead the terrifyingly beautiful seductresses that draw humans into the black underdepths of the sea, and into our own subconscious. And icons are the projections of the gods for whom we are willing to die, but also to kill. The question is not one of belief, but rather, what are the roots of these myths in the human mind?

MacEwen could write: "All our so called consciousness is a more or less fantastic commentary upon an unknown text." The Dutch composer Rudi van Dijk, who set poems from her book *Shadow Maker* to music, claimed that MacEwen had "something in common with Strindberg and D. H. Lawrence as an explorer of these dark corners of the soul that most of us shut out conveniently, in order to create a safe but illusory reality."

The painter Charles Pachter suggested that she could draw you into her fascinations and find a way to make you change your thinking. "Everything was a sensual treat. There was an otherworldliness, an enormous sensitivity and vulnerability to Gwen." There was also a playfulness. Margaret Atwood would say that MacEwen, with her exquisite, porcelain psyche, loved the intersection of the banal and the numinous. "She would come up with the idea that the universe was shaped like a donut and then come up with the name of the brand." A knitting party against the backdrop of the Acropolis is certainly such a juxtaposition.

MacEwen concludes her travelogue with the comment: "In this country you are drawn like a bow between heaven and earth, and you may come to know life and death as one blinding, fluid reality. The soul is the arrow shot from that bow, only once."

Her poem "The White Horse" was written in Greece:

This is the first time you have ever seen
                    your hand, as it is also
The first time you have smelled the blue fire
Within a stone, or tasted blue air, or
Heard what the sea says when it talks in its sleep.

How can we be destroying the world when it is so beautiful! Perhaps we must learn to absorb it imaginatively, as MacEwen did.

Contents

Athens
THE KNITTING PARTY

1

Mycenae
THE GIANTS

17

Mystras
THE SEARCH FOR THE GREAT WHITE HORSE

27

Olympia
THE RUNNERS

43

The Island
A DIARY

55

Stones and Angels
A RETURN TO ATHENS

89

Athens
THE KNITTING PARTY

I REMEMBER the day we all sat in Christina's living room, knitting ourselves into oblivion, the needles sounding to me like insect noises or the strange little chirps of birds. The shoes we had flung off lay there on the floor the way shoes do — gaping open, gasping, staring. There were five of us (or was it six?) all knitting up a storm in the August heat, stopping now and then to mop our brows and sip *limonadha*. Through the slits in the casement window the Acropolis and its temples of sanity hovered in the white, completely non-distorted distance, and a high white wind assailed the stones.

Sophia was knitting a shawl; Irini was doing something I couldn't make out, and the two (or was it three?) others were whipping up baby dresses. I, on the other hand, was not really knitting, for I can't, but I went through the motions and told myself that the results would be a submarine, or possibly a bungalow, or something of that nature. At any rate it would be *effective*. Never having knitted (knat?) in my life, I attempted to hide the fact by clicking crazily and twisting my wrists like a contortionist. I stuffed the results in my handbag the moment they wiggled from the needles, and smiled even when I stabbed myself in the ribs with one of my weapons of domesticity.

Television programs in Greece are quite overwhelming, and I was tempted to stop my work and concentrate on the French tightrope walker who was just then balanced on one foot in the middle of the rope and simultaneously playing *The Saints Go Marching In* on a trombone. God, how we work for our moments of glory. Then a lion-tamer came on and tamed five great beasts who'd probably been doped up especially for the show. Dina let out a whoop of admiration for the lion-tamer's superhuman courage and skill. '*Epeitheno!*' she cried, dropping several stitches in the baby dress. 'Wonderful!'

I meanwhile was more concerned about the lions, poor things, having to trot around the cage and jump over tinsel-papered boxes and roll about on the ground like fools. In dismay, I stabbed myself in my left palm with my knitting needle and felt horrible. Then a bare-chested black man came on and let out spine-chilling and soul-destroying whoops and yells, after which he proceeded to lift a large chair with his bare teeth, and swing it about thirty times around his head — higher, a little higher each time. We made the obvious comments and jokes, such as who his dentist might be, and so forth, but really we were enthralled. I'd seen a chair-lifting stunt in a Greek *taverna* — (a lot of things happen in Greek *tavernas*) — but nothing to rival that.

The circus show went off the air, followed by a terrific soccer game with the Piraeus team battling the Slavs and losing, magnificently. What a fight the Greeks put up when all is lost! Those marvellous agile legs in the long white socks running through all the fields and bloody stadiums of history and winning somehow, even when they lose.

I recalled with half a mind the girl I'd seen some time before, a German tourist, who had jumped into the fountain in Omonia Square in the true tourist tradition. The main idea, of course, being to stop traffic, to be outrageous, to *be*

Greek, whatever she had thought that meant. Non-Greeks tend to have the ridiculous opinion that inspiration is a matter of planned departure from the norm, whatever that is — refusing to understand that real energy, real effervescence springs up spontaneously from the self. So Greece is crowded every summer with eager visitors all trying to play Zorba, and making themselves foolish in the effort. She (the German girl) no doubt had fancied herself as a modern Aphrodite rising from the foam of the Omonia fountain, clogging the traffic in downtown Athens for a full half-hour. Wonderful! With all the coloured lights being turned off, the jetting gush of the water itself, the police fishing her out safely from the murky shallows. And all the Athenians laughing and watching.

The fountain in Omonia Square *is* pretty shallow, and I confess I thought myself more adventurous than the German Aphrodite, as I sank into the fathomless depths of the knitting party and of my thoughts.

What was it Seferis had written?

> *A little further*
> *We will see the almond trees blossoming*
> *the marble gleaming in the sun*
> *the sea breaking into waves*
>
> *a little further*
> *let us rise a little higher*

Greece presents a very real challenge to whoever goes there — a challenge to do more, to be more, to better the present moment in whatever way is possible, to improvise, to expand. To get things *off the ground.*

An incredible spaghetti of strands kept issuing from the needles, most of which I managed to stuff into my bag to avoid detection by the other women. But I knat, I knat like a fiend, and thought of the bitter daphnes blossoming at the edges of the ancient *agora*, rampant and wild with scent as always. Afternoon was leaning on the shoulders of evening, and the man downstairs came in to give us a big bunch of what he called 'night flowers' — a plant which seems to go berserk with fragrance in the darkness and then becomes contrite and bland at dawn. We all inserted our noses into the pungent leaves and sighed. Our visitor stayed for about twenty minutes, chatting about this and that, about nothing and everything. He didn't have to explain his presence or invent an occasion for a visit, the way one so often has to do in the West. In Greece, as in most Mediterranean countries, one drops in on one's neighbours and thus *creates* an occasion. Family members, on the whole, are in very close touch with one another. (Your telephone bill in Greece is based on the number of calls you make; there is no such thing as a flat monthly rate.)

One is never really 'alone' here, I thought. It can be painfully difficult at times to explain one's desire for an hour or so of 'aloneness'; such desires are considered to be essentially anti-social. It is futile to insist that one's work — i.e. painting, writing, studying, etc. — requires concentration, because concentration is also anti-social.

Strands of multi-coloured thoughts and memories kept emerging from my head as I knat and knat. I fancied myself as a kind of Zeus giving birth to Athena from my split skull. Somehow I would have to make order out of my experiences in Greece, even if I couldn't whip up a shawl or a dress with my bare hands. Should I begin, then, with the little Byzantine church on Hermes Street with an entire office building thrown up *around* it, and say that this is the only true meaning of history – mad convergences of cultures and times? Or should I start with the chaos of downtown Athens where kids from Europe and the States wearing Greek village clothes jostle with genuine Greeks wearing the latest things from Europe and the States? (You spot the tourists in Athens by how superficially Greek they try to look.) Or the hundreds of little *souvlaki* stands dispensing deliciously spiced chunks of lamb and veal on sticks with hunks of bread to soak up the juice? Or Monasteraki, much like an oriental bazaar in Cairo or Damascus, where they sell copperware and antique jewellery and rabbit rugs and tapestries and figurines and miniature copies of famous statues and Turkish swords and handmade clothes and silver filigree and paintings and blown-up photos of the Parthenon?

(I'd been lucky in Monasteraki, for I'd been able to haggle in Greek – and no other language is so suited to nagging and haggling – while drinking the *gazoza* generously supplied by the management. I managed nine times out of ten to lower the price of an article by almost half. I used to explain to those delightful shop-owners that my rather odd accent was due to the fact that, though of Greek descent, I was born in Canada and hence had lost touch with my mother tongue. I suspected, though, that we were playing double games – which, by the way, is not at all unethical in the East; in fact it is a social requirement – for although it was plain to me that my story was not believed, it was nevertheless honoured, and I got an *A* for effort every time.)

I shall have to get above all this, I thought, as my bag began to bulge with the hysterical results of my non-knitting. When and if I ever write about Greece I shall begin with something incredible, like the tale of Karaiskakis, the bastard son of a nun from Thessaly who became a hero in 1821 in the war of independence from the Turks. The Acropolis, that bashed-up pinnacle of man's aspirations, had been once destroyed by the Persians, once accidentally blown up by gunpowder, and further bombed by the Turks. But on learning that the Turks were dismantling the columns of Athena's temple to obtain lead for shot from the rods inside, Karaiskakis saw red and dispatched two horses laden with lead up the mountain to supply the enemy so that they would leave the columns alone!

When and if I ever write about Greece I thought, I will pass over briefly, and with shame, the infamous exploits of Lord Elgin ... I will subtly forget to mention how he got permission from the Turks to haul away the famous marbles from the Acropolis, including one of the *karyatid* figures, and later sold the whole lot to the British government. I will openly omit his offer to finance repairs for the *Erechtheum.* (Anyway, his offer was declined, due to the fact that the Turks feared that the 'infidels' who would set up the scaffolding would cast heathen eyes upon the gorgeous harem which had taken up quarters within the venerable walls.)

When and if I ever write about Greece, I thought, I will begin with the dark Gypsies in the square in Kipseli, wearing carnival masks and selling little plastic pictures of saints to the coffee-drinkers in the outdoor cafés. I will proceed from the lovely *tzigana* who approached me with a baby at her breast, its head covered with horrid red scabs. I gave her all my silver, and thought it was not enough, and people told me after that it was a hundred times more than I should have given. 'These *ghifti*,' they said, (using the derogatory word for 'Gypsies'), 'You don't ever know who's the real mother. This woman you saw, she will pass on the child to a different woman to parade around in another place, another square.'

And I had wondered what difference that made – *who* paraded the little thing around. Scabs were scabs, money was money, and food was food. What particular systems the Gypsy women worked out among themselves didn't really interest me. What had caught my attention was the fact that although that particular *tzigana* had lowered her voice in a kind of whine to ask for my help, her head, nevertheless, had been held very high.

At first I found the attitude of the Greeks towards Gypsies terribly indifferent, and it disturbed me. But then, I thought, I carried money with me at all times, and not everybody did, or could. Greek generosity for the most part centres around the home; it is widely extended to anyone within the particular social or family circuit, and it is lavishly extended towards foreigners, as everywhere in the East. But the Gypsy is neither family nor foreigner; he is a known entity, neither inside nor completely outside the social or family circuit. To the Greeks, I think, he is a dim reminder of the almost indescribable hungers and tribulations which they themselves suffered countless times at the hands of conquerors and occupiers of their land. Those Greeks who now enjoy a relative prosperity in the big cities are very often the same people, or descendants of same, who knew fearful hunger during the German occupation of Greece, or whose forefathers knew it still more during the years following the war of freedom from the Turks. Could I have given away my *drachmas* so easily to a needy person, had I been a woman from a remote village who had learned to save every ounce of soup for her children? Would I invent ridiculous tales of the Gypsies' deception if every single coin I owned in my life was there to serve my immediate family? Would I even have the *time* to ponder over such matters, had I lived through the birth-pangs of a struggling new nation, the civil wars, the sheer horror of the last hundred years?

I shall have to get above all this, I thought, as Dina switched the TV program to *Mannix*, with dubbed-in Greek soundtrack. That veritable American non-man began threatening gangsters at gun-point in the language of the gods. What am I doing here? I thought, as I glanced down to the sea where an American battleship was anchored, casting off what looked like inter-galactic signals in the purple dark.

Blue- and yellow-eyed cats were scrounging the alleyways and garbage cans for scraps of meat. Scared to death at the sight of man, they fled into the charcoal dark whenever someone approached them. In Greece, the only thing to do with animals is eat them, ride them or abuse them. This is the result of too many years of deprivation, too much hunger. In the West, we've had time to consider our roles in the physical world, and we've come to certain belated, but important ecological conclusions. In countries like Greece there has simply not been enough time, peacetime, for people to consider such things as the overpopulation of the planet, the importance of Vitamin E in nutrition, and whether or not animals have souls. In recent centuries there has been no time for Greece to cast its eyes outward, to see what else is alive, and frightened, and in pain in the world.

History has made beasts of us all. But that only makes sense when we consider that we beasts made history. As Seferis wrote, we shall have to rise *a little higher* — meaning, I think, we shall have to get things *off the ground.*

There is something vastly unreal about the Acropolis lit by night; it is the same unreality that surrounds two other 'high places' I have seen which have become the victims of the hellish *son et lumière* shows — the fortress of Saladin in Cairo and the great pyramids in Giza. Huxley maintained in *The Doors of Perception* that modern artificial lighting allows us to appreciate ancient architecture and sculpture in new and thrilling ways. For me, however, those huge waves of unreal light create a nightmarish quality I can do without. When the Parthenon was built, nobody anticipated that one day hundreds of viewers would sit entranced before its holy pillars, half blinded not by the light of God but by that of Edison. Some things can only be understood in pure sunlight or in the discreet illumination of torches.

I didn't really want to get into a long conversation with the girls about why I hated the sight of the Acropolis by night, so I turned away from the window and imagined I could hear the strident notes from the *bouzoukia* of Plaka — the night-spots which form a weird, winding network of music and laughter along the lower slopes of the mountain of the Acropolis. Above, in the Parthenon, the freaky stillness of history. Below, a maze of streets full of cafés, *boîtes, tavernas,* each competing with the other for the right to do permanent damage to the human ear. And yet, often, hidden away in a dark corner under a roof of lattice-work and grapevines, the surprise: the lone *santouri* player caressing the countless strings of his instrument upon the table.

I suppose I was enjoying the knitting party. Maria had left with her little boy. Irini was falling asleep under the icon of Saint Nikolaus. The television was now presenting a young Greek singer wandering through rows of papier-maché Doric columns and looking for his inevitable *agape.* 'My love, my love,' he sang.

I suppose I was enjoying the knitting party while it lasted, because I knew the next day I would have to go downtown and obtain some paper or permit which would allow me to go somewhere or do something. The government offices like something out of Kafka, the office clerks brandishing their ball-point pens like swords. Pictures of Jesus Christ and Papadoupoulos smiling enigmatically from behind the filing cabinets and desks. Two, three, sometimes four hours of waiting. Wondering if Christ with His upraised hand had the papers. Wondering what the papers were for. The posters all over Greece praising the government, the army, the children, and God....

I dozed over my knitting. I dreamed of the Roman *agora* and a drinking trough for ancient horses, the water still trickling from a secret source in the rock and forming a stagnant pool full of hornets and bugs and turtles. The Greek *agora*, and the path among the bitter daphnes past the great *stoa*. The fallen marble slabs and semi-walls which had been offices and courts of law. (Red tape, red stone.) The three giant statues who are snake-men and fish-men and beautifully unholy there against the glaring sky. Climbing the steps to the Thesion, and the air alive with cicadas. Graffiti from the 18th Century on the temple walls, and not a dirty word to be found.

A deep well where I looked down into the darkness and almost found myself ...

My handbag fell on the floor and the mad macaroni of my knitting emerged. No one noticed, and I grabbed it up. I made small talk, whatever that is, to avoid blurting out the tale of my archeological discoveries at an unexcavated wall at Keramikos. I'd found bits of real Roman glass and black shards; I'd dug them out with my bare hands and stuffed them into my pockets.

But Dina and Irini and Christina and Sophis would have laughed at the tale. These women had no need to collect tokens of history; they knew how to knit past and future into the gaudy and complex patterns of the living present. In their devotion to the present, they create history. Not me, I thought. I'll never learn to knit. Like the time I triumphantly showed my hostess an enormous piece of an archaic *amphora* which I'd acquired from a fisherman who'd dragged it out of the sea. Seeing the hideous black salt-encrusted thing, she let out a little cry and said, 'My God, what broke?'

I laughed and laughed at that. How marvellously right on
was her reaction – the reaction of someone whole and
unbroken, with little need to dwell upon the shards of the
past. I on the other hand had spent hours puzzling over
certain things in the Athens Museum, assuming I could
somehow impose an order on those relics, a continuity of
meaning which would suit *me*. Trying to bridge the gap
between the stiff and disagreeable *kouroi* figures to the
stunning bronze Poseidon who stands on a pedestal in what
is perhaps the most exquisitely-balanced stance ever
achieved in sculpture. Not being able, though, to understand
how a mere few hundred years could have brought about
such a development in style. Fishing around for soothing
explanations, and finding none. The truth, of course, being
hopelessly simple, which is why I don't have a clue as to
what it might be.

The archaic figures from the Cyclades astonished me.
They are white, highly-stylized pieces showing only the
merest suggestion of the human form. One of them, a
statuette of a musician dating back to about 2300 B.C. is so
lyrical in line, curving and looping about in unexpected directions, and so utterly whimsical that I wanted to laugh out
loud when I first saw it. It has been suggested that Cycladic
artists could not portray the human form accurately – a
notion which I'm sure is rubbish. They portrayed animals
with incredible accuracy, and it seems that they had *fun* with
human anatomy, almost in the same way a modern artist
might. In any case, they knew exactly what they were doing.

The transition from the Greek to the Roman galleries in
the Museum was depressing. *Here we are*, I thought. Here is
the birth of Western Man. A whole new breed of human
being. Gone is the subtle Greek smile, the inner knowledge
– and in its place the hard, ironic features of the new masters
of the world with their vacant yet disturbing eyes. The new

worldliness and cynicism around the mouths. The conquerors, whose brittle power was won at the expense of
something infinitely more powerful and delicate. The loss is
there on all the Roman faces. The bewilderment. The dark,
the bitter knowledge that the future was theirs, yet it meant
nothing.

I shook myself out of my reveries. I realized that I had
knat a whole row of something which held together in a
feeble sort of way, and Sophia cried, '*Kalitera*, Gwendolyn!'
I was getting better.

A fervent involvement with the present moment is one of
the things that makes the Greeks so Greek. An almost
ferocious attention given to whatever one is doing at any
given time. The intensity of emotion which is a result of this
can be often overwhelming and exhausting. You find yourself getting momentarily, but deeply involved with store-
owners and cab-drivers when discussing some minor affair
or problem. Small talk is fraught with heavy emotional
overtones, and the simplest point must often be gotten
across with hands and arms gesticulating all over the place.
You start punctuating your spoken sentences with dramatic
gestures and facial expressions you never knew you pos-
sessed. But what is more important, and just as directly
related to the involvement with the present moment — is
that you find yourself constantly called upon, in almost
every situation, to rise above yourself. To do more, to *be*
more, as I have said before. The Greeks live in a state of
tension which to others may resemble madness. At the very
least, it is bewildering. Or glorious. It depends on who you
are, and how real you like your reality.

One of the most intense people I ever met in Greece was a
little hunchbacked girl who came to my table in the café in

Omonia Square, holding a box to collect money. I went through the usual spasms of pity — (embarrassment in disguise) — until I noticed that she had one of the liveliest faces I'd ever seen. She said she really enjoyed meeting all the wonderful people in the cafés at night. She also collected match-boxes from all over the world, and would I please send her one with a beaver or a maple-leaf from Canada. Spiritually, she was one of the healthiest people I've seen. No one had ever destroyed her youthfulness by suggesting that begging was a sin or shame.

The poor and the ill carry no social stigmata in Greece. They are people with a different set of circumstances. They do not beg; they ask for assistance, and generally they get it. The word 'neurosis', which ironically stems from the Greek, has little or no meaning in Greece itself. Nerves, yes. Neurosis, no.

Neurosis will come when the tentacles of the American octopus slither into every dark corner of the East. At the moment there's just the big fat head of the beast lurking in the Mediterranean waiting. The Big Powers play chess with the so-called 'emerging nations', and Spiro Agnew manages to sputter a feeble *'efkharisto poli' (thank you very much)*, to the Greek people. Sometimes, though, a single pawn in a chess game decides the match, and Greece holds a pawn which the new Romans have not even thought of.

A Fred Astaire film came on television, and Christina went out into the garden to feed the doves in their big wire cage. Despite the blare of the TV, a quietness had come over the night and I went out into the garden to breathe the blossomy air. The smell reminded me of the little church where I'd been only a few days before. The body of the poet George Seferis had lain there for a day, surrounded by flowers. I had wanted to meet him when I went to Athens, but he had died on me, and I stood in the church before the coffin, wondering why everything was so dark inside, while outside the Greek sun was flooding the streets with light.

I had gone up to the Acropolis after paying my respects to the dead poet. I was sweating like a horse after the steep climb, and Seferis' words circled in my memory, as the light banged against the ancient pillars:

> *a little further*
> *let us rise a little higher*

And there in a high white wind among the stones I imagined for a moment that I knew exactly what he had meant in those lines.

When I went back indoors all the women were gone, taking their day's work with them — shawls and socks and baby dresses, and God knows what. The knitting party was over.

Mycenae
THE GIANTS

T HE windows of the night train revealed a landscape almost lunar in its starkness. The train hugged a wall of rock made steel blue by midnight; the mountainside had the consistency of quicksilver. When we passed over the bridge at the great canal of Corinth, we seemed to be suspended in a hunk of purple midnight space. Everything dwarfed us. We were on our way to Mycenae.

The next morning, rainwater turned red as blood in the hollows of the stones in Corinth. Nikos and I stood in the ancient *agora* and gazed up at the mountain where holy whores once had their temple; a Byzantine castle now clings precariously to the summit. Everything's so *big* in this country, I thought. What is it? Everything's stretching and reaching and gasping for more and more space. The infamous light seems to yank things out of their contexts and present them naked and fullblown to the eye. Everything demands attention; there is nothing subtle about Greece.

Mountain water still trickled through one of the great underground tunnels at the fountain of Pirene, reminding us of the fluidity of time. I wanted to go down the steps which led to a sacred spring, but the gate at the bottom was closed. I wanted to climb Parnassus, snow-capped in the distance, but it was too far away. I wanted everything; I wanted to be enormous and overwhelming, yawning and expansive like the light.

We moved on to the town of Argos, ate, and got a ride into Naphlion where we intended to stay the night. As we drove along the lazy Argive plain — (I believe that's what they say in travel books) — Nikos suddenly leaned out of the window, gave a cry of surprise, and told the driver to turn around.

'What is it?' I asked.

'I think we should stop,' said Nikos. 'We've just hit Tiryns. I forgot it was here.'

'We've just hit *what!*' I cried, marvelling at the colossal coolness of his statement, for Tiryns was the second gigantic stronghold of the ancient Greeks, sister city to Mycenae. 'Where is it? Why can't I see it?'

'It's back a bit from the road,' he said.

The driver turned off onto a smaller road and the walls of the great fortress came into view. It was late afternoon and the sky was turning greenish-grey, announcing rain.

'My God,' I said feebly as we got out of the car. 'This place must have been built by giants.'

'There are legends about that,' Nikos said. 'Some people still believe them.'

Dark clouds were scuttling across the changing sky, and the huge walls of Tiryns looked darker and more menacing than I ever would have imagined. The fortress seemed to be a somber, mighty statement of sheer brute strength, of sheer size in the face of our littleness. The enormous stones seemed to smirk at us as we walked along the ancient pathways. We were puny, ridiculous; *we* had not built this place. And yet it had a kind of bulky, awesome beauty like a sound idea blown out of all proportion, like a symphony which is too long.

I shivered. The sky was very dark now, and the first drops of rain struck the monstrous stones. We left at the first sound of thunder, and when we looked back, Tiryns was a great grey elephant asleep on the horizon. It rained all the way into Naphlion.

I think it was Saturday when we went to Mycenae. I can't be sure, but I'm going by the feeling that certain days have certain colours, and this was a blonde day – dusty blonde, to be more precise. The air smelled of ancient, unknown flowers, and all the cicadas were singing like mad in the groves in the hollows of the hills. The rise in the land was so gradual that we didn't realize how high we were until we reached the ruins of the ancient city and heard the high dry wind whistling around the circular walls.

'Giants built this place,' I whispered, as we approached the Lion's Gate. Nikos just smiled, and ran his hand along one of the great blonde stones.

I looked up and there they were – the two splendid equivocal lions gracing the gate of the fabulous city, gazing at one another as they had gazed for more than three and a half thousand years. The double beast which, like the two-headed eagle of the Byzantines, I had always imagined to symbolize the dual nature of human existence – free will, and Fate. For a moment I could see the tragic Orestes standing where we stood, contemplating a horrendous matricide, struggling to rationalize his actions in terms of the dictates of his own mind rather than those of divine law. A few lines from a long poem, *Orestes*, by the Greek poet Yannis Ritsos came to my mind.

And now,
in front of this gate I feel totally unready; —
the two marble lions — see them? — they've grown tame,
they, who started out so dauntless when we were children,
half wild, their manes bristling for some foolhardy leap,
now finally settled down agreeably on the top corners of the gate
with dead hair, vacant eyes, — terrifying nobody, — wearing
    an expression
of punished dogs, bearing no resentment,
their tongues licking from time to time the warm soles of night.

We passed through the gate and entered the ruins of the city of Agamemnon, a city once stuffed with gold from the spoils of war, from the conquest of Troy, a city which now exists only in the mind and in the mute stones where snails and snakes and lizards go about their furtive business. Nothing is left except golden coins and ornaments in the museum in Athens, and the famous masks, all flattened out and funny in the daze of death, to tell us what really happened here. A great city rose and fell; it's an old, old story.

We need our giants, I thought bleakly as I stood over the royal graveyard. Mighty kings with glittering plans and abysmally cunning minds were buried here, in this snail-like, circular Necropolis. They are gone, poof, vanished. History is merely history; it is only glorified through myth.

I joined Nikos, who had gone on ahead of me and was standing at the far side of the ruins, looking over the sheer drop down the mountainside. Beyond, a sister mountain glowing with gold and mauve seemed so close we might have reached out and touched it. The mighty sky was also a tangible thing — a dome of glass. Dizziness made us draw back and continue our wanderings among the stones.

We came across the entrance to an enormous underground cistern which must have been one of the reservoirs
of water for the city in times of siege. We descended, daring
each other at every step, for the ancient slippery stairs were
worn down by centuries of feet making their way deeper and
deeper into the bowels of the mountain. It was pitch black
and dreadfully chill. It was terrifying. Somehow it seemed to
me to be a place of death, although I could not think why. It
was a place of water, and water is life ... and yet somewhere
at the very bottom of that reservoir a single drop of water
was going *tinkle tinkle,* and sending up black, distorted rings
of sound which were almost visible. I remembered Rider
Haggard's *She,* and the nightmare of immortality. The
worn-down stairs, the sad passageways in the caves of Kôr. I
brooded over the evils of Time.

Later we took pictures of one another standing in the
cone-shaped archway at the far end of the city. It was
constructed with the same unbelievably huge blocks of stone
as the Lion's Gate. We wondered if it might have been a sort
of back door to the city, an emergency exit in times of siege.
Whatever it was, it made us look like pygmies. Mycenae
really cuts you down to size.

Finally we went to the place alternately known as the
Treasury of Atreus or the grave of Agamemnon, a curious,
beehive-shaped structure cut into a hillside. Once inside, a
strange trick of acoustics distorted human voices, so that
they seemed to be coming from within the very walls.
People stood around in small groups, speaking in hushed
whispers, giggling nervously now and again as the walls
giggled back. We didn't stay long.

As we drove away from Mycenae the afternoon light was
turning from gold to copper, and the city looked serene and
mysterious, as though it held some brilliant secret — perhaps
at the bottom of that dark cistern — which would never be

brought to light.

Nikos was laughing silently as we turned a bend in the road and the city was lost from view.

'What's funny?' I asked.

'Giants,' he replied. 'Giants are funny.'

'They are not. They're serious. And anyway, I like them,' I said.

It was dusk when we returned to Naphlion.

The next day we went to Epidaurus to see the ancient theatre which once seated fifteen thousand people who chattered and munched cheese and olives, scolded their children, laughed at the plays of Aristophanes, wept at the tragedies of Euripides and generally, no doubt, had a fabulous time. It is situated in a marvellous grove of pines and red leafy vines which give off burning, pungent aromas. We walked through the ruins of the temple of Aesculapius and the surrounding ruins which were all part of a great medical centre of the ancient world. People came here for cures for every conceivable disease of the body or the mind. I shuddered when we came to a structure known as the *tholos* of Polycleites – a sort of circular labyrinth whose function is still not entirely clear. Some say it was used for secret religious initiations; others say it may have been a prison (or even a bank!). But the most probable theory is that it was used for curing certain types of insanity, the idea being that the patient underwent some sort of experience in the labyrinth so fearful that it snapped him back to reality. It is always associated with snakes, and one wonders if the idea was to cure mental disease by employing the very symbol of all that is loathsome and fearful in the human unconscious, to lead the patient through, as it were, the labyrinth of his own mind. The symbol of medicine is still a serpent coiled around a staff. In any case, we did not like the *tholos*, and we moved on.

The air was wild with the smell of mustard and pines. We sat in the top row of the ancient theatre and listened while a man far down below us dropped a single *drachma* onto the dot that indicated centre stage. Like a pebble dropped into a still pool, the coin made tinkling rings of pure sound which rose to greet us through the hot blonde air.

'Nikos,' I said. 'I just had a thought. What if they *weren't* giants? I mean the builders of Mycenae. What if they were just like us, you know, hopelessly mortal and all that, clipping their fingernails, worrying about their grey hairs, troubled by their nightmares....'

Nikos laughed. 'You build big when you're scared,' he said. 'And they built *big!*'

I thought about that for a while, and gradually it all made sense. 'So,' I whispered sadly, 'They weren't giants after all, were they? They were just plain scared.'

'Scared silly, I would say,' he said.

God, the price we pay for our illusions. Someone dropped another coin onto centre stage and the air turned silver.

Mystras

THE SEARCH FOR THE GREAT WHITE HORSE

W E streamed down the mountain from Tripoli in cold driving rain, on the trail of Constantine Palaeologus, last of the Byzantine emperors. We had heard (read?) (dreamed?) that his spirit still hovered over the city of Mystras, and that it had been known to appear in the guise of a great white horse on the deserted mountain stronghold. It seemed so important to us to discover the great lords, the dead ones — for they dwell in us still; their voices clamour in the night, they charge through our sleep like stallions.

So we went after the phantom beast, or the Emperor himself, whichever we would find.

To be as blindly specific as possible — we streamed down the mountain from Tripoli, and our cab driver who loved us more than life itself demonstrated the fact by taking the hairpin turns with a smiling nonchalance which chilled our blood. He informed us meanwhile that of all the people he had taken to Mystras, we were the first who wanted to go there to find a horse.

His name was George — *the* George, as they say in Greek, since all names in Greek are preceded by the definite article to make one feel like a being rather than a word — and we had discovered him in Naphlion drinking *gazoza* beside his cab stand and more than willing to take us to some of the more inaccessible parts of the Peloponnese.

Horrors of mist, sheer drops into raining nothingness awaited us at each bend in the mountain road. The mind gets used to such things, though the body curls up into a tight knot of terror and stays that way all down to the Acadian plain of sheep and goats and apples and tons of red, red earth. And from there even lower into Sparta, through narrow foggy valleys and passes, which, in the dark unreal rain, gave me a ghastly *déjà vu*.

You can't really begin to *think* in Greece until things get dark. It's the rain, or the dusk, or perhaps even a cloud or two which brings things into a reasonable perspective. All those tons of sunlight hammering away at the pillars of the Acropolis make history too lucid to be real, and you begin to wonder if light itself is a lie, a bright guise of God, not an illumination. And maybe darkness is better, the darkness in which Constantine died, the dark end of the Byzantine Empire....

He was crowned on the 6th of January, 1449, in Mystras, provincial stronghold of the Empire, capital city of the Despotate of the Peloponnese. Then he went to Constantinople and died. In his life he defended what was left of the Empire, which was not much, for when he took the throne the Empire had to all intents and purposes fallen.

Through the Spartan plain, the rain still freezing, and ahead of us at last the abandoned phantom city.

'*Panagea mou!*' whispered the George. 'Isn't it beautiful!' and put his foot on the accelerator to bring us closer. The Greeks do not linger over beauty; they devour it.

Nikos said nothing and I merely murmured an ineffectual 'Wow', for I had had a glimpse of Mystras and it seemed to me to be some incredible *thing*, beast or plant, all in frag-

ments and clinging to the˙ mountainside the way a
nightmare clings to the mind of a sleeper. It was ghastly,
green with rain, tragic with history, unspeakably *Byzantine*.

We had to pass through the modern village at the foot of
the mountain. Here were the descendants of the people who
had gradually abandoned the ancient stronghold to live in
relative peace in the Spartan plain, having had their fill of
Franks and Turks and who knows what else history had
served them up both before and after Constantine. I was
tempted to stop and ask one of them if they knew anything
of the legend of the great white horse, but a shyness held me
back. We slowed down, though, at a statue in the town
square.

'Who's that?' the George asked one of the passersby, a
small boy carrying a white goat on his shoulders.

'Oh *him*,' the boy smiled. 'That's Constantine.'

As we pulled away I tried to get a good look at the features
of the statue, but I saw only an over-large metallic king with
an amazingly determined face. He was dressed for war. I had
expected him to be wearing a thin tubular Byzantine cos-
tume with little pointed slippers — like the ones you see on
playing cards — but I suppose he only wore such things for
religious ceremonies and public festivals. He had a beard, I
think. And a helmet. I thought that since he had been
crowned in January it would have been raining then too....

Most of the older men of the village were in the café — or
café-neon as they say — drinking coffee or *ouzo* at that hour
of the day, and as we passed through the narrow streets we
heard their coaxing, argumentative voices, and the occa-
sional clicking of the dice on the *tavali* boards.

The entrance to the phantom city was freezing stone. The
trees wailed with cold, and I feared that the entire stronghold
would somehow lose its grip on the mountainside and slide
down into oblivion in a gush of mud and agony. But we paid

our ten *drachmas* to the guard at the gate – a sullen fellow who was fortified on that particular day with a hefty bottle of *Metaxa* brandy – bought two guide-books which got immediately soaked, covered our heads with the latest newspapers from Athens, and passed out from under the arch.

Nikos uttered an exclamation of alarm. We had expected a ghost town, but this was ridiculous. It took us a while to comprehend what was confronting us – not a smallish wreck of a Byzantine stronghold, but an *entire city*, absolutely abandoned and broken. A city which wound up and up the mountainside in a steep maze which mocked our wildest dreams. The rain assaulted the cobblestones, the skeletons of mansions, the countless arches, the monasteries and chapels, the granaries, the palace of the Palaeologoi. And finally, on the very top, the castle which we had to bend over backwards to see. It dawned on me – (strange how the obvious dawns on you at times like these) – that they built castles on the tops of mountains so nobody could *reach* them.

In a limp attempt to bring things down to earth, I muttered 'Where's the George?' and imagined to my horror that our mad friend had driven up the highway to await us at the castle gate, the last exit of Mystras, the absolute top, from which, for some obscure reason, he figured we would triumphantly emerge.

Our guide-books had turned to soup in our hands, and we flung them away, enraged. I noticed on the pavement one half-readable page – a diagram, a map of Mystras of such complex character that it would require two weeks of intensive study to comprehend. Where *were* we? The place needed a month, a year, ten years to understand, and we had a couple of hours. In dark rain. Newspapers on our heads. Frozen to the bone. The latest news from Athens slowly dripping into my hair – who got out of jail, who got put in, reasons for same, ecstatic anticipations of the forthcoming visit of Spiro Agnew, and ads for Vim detergent.

We became depressed; the city overpowered us. We slid accidentally into the courtyard of a church, having lost all hope of ever finding the great white horse.

But then I saw him.

Not the horse, but *him*, Constantine, dressed in a long red tubular robe with pointed slippers. I saw his crown, his face, everything. The rain was a million bullets on the mosaic floor. I saw the drinking-place for the horses, I saw his retinue entering the chapel with heavy soaked velvet clothes, I saw the gilded priests crowning the last of the Palaeologoi, at the close of an empire.

And the ghastly rain kept falling, falling, and the ikons in the chapel were purple with cold. A purple mountain rose up behind us and the last Lord of the Byzantines was falling, falling to his knees before the golden faces of the Virgin and the Child, accepting the crown of a hopeless empire upon his head.

I stood in the doorway of the chapel, gazing first into the cold sanctuary of Christ, and then out into the pounding courtyard where the emperor trod in his little golden slippers, where the hooves of his horses trod, and the heavy boots of his endless guards.

All this is history, but it was only much later that I learned that out of all the countless churches and chapels in Mystras, it was this one, Saint Demetrius, which had been chosen for the coronation. This is accident, or miracle. I merely record what I saw.

Back out, then, into the everlasting deluge, coldest day of our lives, cursing the George who had abandoned us for the impossible heights of Mystras, the summit, the last refuge in times of siege. Sliding through arched avenues, peering despondently into abandoned homes. On a green patch of field a monstrous jungle-plant clung to the earth dripping rain like sweat. Barbaric greenery, and beneath, in the grass and rocks, the hugest snails in the world, closed now in their armoured shells, little fortresses of horror threatening at any moment to open.

Soaked to the soul, still we searched for the great white horse, but all we could see through the insane rain was the little playing-card king slipping and sliding ahead of us, flanked by guards and aides, all of them like us cursing the cold and the cobblestones. Constantine (perhaps?) cursing his own coronation and the empire he had to uphold, a thing which had crumbled before he was even born.

We had only covered about one one-hundredth of the city before we knew we would have to give up and go back to the main gate. The chill in our bones was the chill of history, the endless sieges of Mystras, assassinations, slaughters. I began to see children's eyes staring out from vaulted doorways, and black-robed women clutching ikons of the Virgin to their breasts, praying for the relief of the city. I imagined the aristocracy up on the higher, safer slopes, perhaps under the protection of the palace or the castle, while the poor got butchered in their flimsy homes or in the streets by invading armies. I kept seeing the rain of war falling, falling. History like a great mud-slide; human beings, snails, donkeys, plants all clutching the mountainside for dear life.

Where the hell was the George? He could save us from these thoughts if only he'd realize that we would emerge from the main gate, and not the top. We tried to get help from the guard, who had sadly slipped more or less under his desk from the effects of the *Metaxa*, but who managed, nevertheless, to put through a call to the summit gate. Whoever was in charge up there, though, had seen neither a car nor a George and had no idea what we were talking about.

'George, you, you jest of God!' I cried — (when I get mad I

am very literary) — and madly flailed the air with what was left of the newspaper from Athens until it dropped in a pulp to the ground.

The guard smiled at us and shrugged his shoulders and gradually slid away from view. Mystras was slowly beginning to slide down the mountain — or so it looked to our feverish eyes. I peered out through the gate, down to the Spartan plain, and tried to imagine the ancient warriors taking winter baths in the Eurotas river. The thought warmed me a little.

We decided to make a mad dash down to the little restaurant called *Marmora* at the foot of the mountain and wait for the George there. The place, as it turned out, was full of British tourists — an odd group which called themselves the Wings, or the Eagles, or something like that. The members all seemed to be well over sixty, and they were soaked to the skin. It seemed obvious that they had attempted to Do Mystras, and failed.

Their leader, who resembled James Mason, and who wore a little emblem of a Wing (or was it an Eagle?) on his blazer, was beamingly addressing the dazed group. 'I must say,' he began, 'The weather *is* rather bad, don't you think? But let's look on the bright side of things, shall we?'

One very old fellow who had fallen asleep with his arms on the table looked up in horror at this remark.

'What I *think* we should do is this. Or rather, one or the other of *these*. That is, in fact: *A* We can proceed to tackle Mystras *regardless*, thus keeping to our original plan which involves pushing on to the caves tomorrow. Or — and this is *B* — we can all go back and have tea in Sparta, and Do Mystras tomorrow, in which case we must forfeit the *caves* and push on later to Olympia. At any rate, I leave the question with you and trust you will come to a decision among yourselves.'

He left off speaking and sat down at his special table — (all

tour leaders seem to have special tables, for some reason) —
with an intriguing-looking German lady who seemed to be a
leader too, except that she didn't have a group.

'Caves, caves!' cried the gentleman who kept falling asleep
over the table, as the group plunged into a heated debate on
the best course of action.

'I say, I think we're doing this all *wrong*,' murmured an
octogenarian in a bowler hat.

Eventually the group decided on tea in Sparta and the
forfeiture of the caves. Wise choice, I thought, as I downed
some brandy and proceeded to become very worried about
the George. Might he have had an accident in the blinding
rain? I dreamed up awful possibilities of what might have
befallen him, realizing that, after all, he had been a great
guy, a paragon of a cab driver, a gentleman and a friend.

— At which point, precisely, the George came strolling
into the restaurant, perfectly dry and crisp, not a hair of his
head out of place, and asked us where we had been.

'George!' I cried with utter relief, flailing the air with my
celery stick and making threatening jabs in his direction.
'What happened? Did you meet the great white horse?'

The next day the snails came out of their shells. We had
spent the night in Sparta and returned to Mystras early in
the morning. The rain had stopped, but the ground was still
chill and damp; the sky was fraught with windblown clouds
and patches of a frightening kind of blue. The first snail I saw
was in the doorway of the mansion of Lascaris; the thing was
sitting there, protruding more than halfway out of its shell,
green and bilious, possibly the most hideous thing I'd ever
seen. The same green as the ghastly jungle plant with its
tendrils clinging to the slope, the turgid green of too much
rain and history.

Nikos and the George began collecting snails, for it turned out that there were hundreds of them, giant ones, naked and exposed in the wet grass. They carried them in hand-kerchiefs and the handkerchiefs squirmed. The floors of the Lascaris mansion almost crumbled as we walked on them, and there were great holes underfoot through which we saw the cellars. A black nun was coming down the mountain leading a donkey laden with baskets; we realized that there *were* a few human inhabitants in Mystras – in the monas-tery of the Pantanassa higher up on the slopes. She greeted us with a very soft *kali mera,* then lowered her eyes and went on her way. The smell of wild mustard and thyme was everywhere, turning the air yellow and green.

In the chapel of the Pantanassa there were frescoed figures of saints with their eyes hacked out. The expungement was the work of Turks who, with their Moslem fear of images, wished to rid the figures of their holy power. They didn't realize that the eyeless faces would become, in some strange way, even more powerful and compelling than ever.

As we were leaving the Pantanassa we saw, as an appar-ition, the octogenarian with the bowler hat hobbling down the road from the castle, clutching a cane and a guide-book. He must have somehow broken away from the Wings (or the Eagles) who were Doing Mystras from the bottom up, and decided to proceed from the summit down. Someone must have driven him up to the summit gate by the main road. His eyes were red and watery from trying to make a safe descent on the treacherously slippery cobblestones, and at the same time from trying to make sense of the cryptic map of Mystras which the guide-book offered.

He paused a moment with his cane uplifted, pointing in the general direction of the Pantanassa. Then he checked the map. 'Ahhh-*ha!*' he said, with a deep sigh of satisfaction, and hobbled vaguely towards his goal. 'Nevertheless,' we heard him mutter as he turned a steep corner in the road. 'I somehow feel I've done this all *wrong*.'

How he had ever made it alone down from the castle is something we shall never know. We only got as high as the palace, from which point the castle stronghold could be seen perched on the dizzying summit far above us.

And still no sign of the great white horse.

At a bend in the road leading to the palace, I felt invisible archers watching us from behind the walls – and as it turned out, there was a narrow vertical slit in one part of the fortifications which must have served as a bowman's lookout. Anyone approaching the palace could have easily been picked off by the sentry who had full visual command of that part of the road. And we – the new invaders – might have been shot by an arrow of mist from the bow of some ghostly archer who'd held his post for five hundred years.

If ever the great white horse would appear, it must be *here*, I thought, as we entered the gates of the palace. Here on the windy heights in the skeleton of Constantine's royal house – a long lonely bunch of arches and walls without roofs. Here with the wild changing sky above, with crazy-horse clouds charging over the Spartan plain against a background of vivid blue. Here where the eternal snails, ugly predators, smirked in the slippery grass. Constantine may have eaten *escargots,* safe within the walls of his palace while outside the wars raged on and the bowmen shot everybody who came up the royal road and failed to give the password. I imagined him sitting at a hewn wood table in mid-winter with a great fire going, his plate heaped with dozens of the beastly things all done up in tomato sauce and onions, like the ones I had once in Athens, or perhaps stuffed with spices and butter, European style. The zing of arrows down below, and lower still the poor people praying in the chapel of Saint Demetrius or huddling in doorways in the rain.

But this is all wrong; Constantine wasn't sitting and eating within the palace walls in wartime. He was out fighting the invaders — the invaders who wear the same faces, always, regardless of who they are.

The George was tired of carrying his handkerchief of snails around, so he dropped the whole thing onto the ground and left the beasts to fend for themselves. We lost him again as he went behind the palace to hunt for herbs or something. When he emerged, immaculate as ever, we made our way back down the maze of roads, and he spoke for the first time in hours. 'History is wonderful! *Panagea mou*, history is really wonderful! Imagine — they all lived here, and worked and ate and died, just as we live and work and eat and die. They were *like us*. It breaks the mind just thinking of it!'

We stopped then, realizing we had taken a wrong turn somewhere in the maze and had 'done the whole thing all wrong'; we had to wind our way back to what looked like a main road, which took a full ten minutes, because we had somehow gotten over to the other side of the mountain.

Panagea mou, I thought (which translates as 'my all-holy one', meaning the Blessed Virgin Mary. Some Greeks pepper their speech with this epithet, as we do ours with 'Oh God', to express the whole range of emotions.) Where is the great white horse, and why hasn't he appeared to us pilgrims who have come so far to find him?

'George,' I asked, 'What do you think about the great white horse?'

'The villagers will know,' he said.

'Will the guard at the gate know?' I asked.

'The guard at the gate knows nothing,' said the George with venom. 'He is a fool, one of the great mistakes of God, a fool and a fiend. We won't ask him.'

I made no comment. The streets had dried out by now and

the stone had been restored to its original colours – pink and beige. Someone had flung an empty pack of Players into the courtyard of Saint Demetrius and my eyes went red with indignation. I remembered a poignant comment a little girl I knew had made about the basic difference between her life in Canada and her life in Greece. 'In Canada I used to get mad,' she said. 'But here – I get *really* mad!'

'We forgot to see the Aphendiko,' I said, stopping in my tracks and remembering an excerpt from the guide-book. 'The place where they have the pictures of the miracles of Christ. The Good Samaritan, The Wedding at Cana, The Healing of The Man With Dropsy, The Healing of The Blind Man, and The Healing of Peter's Mother-In-Law.'

'Nobody could heal Peter's mother-in-law,' said the George grimly. 'I know.'

As we left through the main gate, he flung the guard a foul look. I learned later that the previous day's episode in the rain had left them with an enduring hatred for one another. The George swore in the name of everything holy that he had left a message with the fellow to inform us of where he would be waiting. The guard, on the other hand, swore in the name of everything holy that he knew nothing of it.

We got into the freezing cab and made our way down to the serene village of Mystras at the foot of the mountain. As we turned a bend in the road, I looked back once and saw the crazy city clinging to the slopes. There was a small grey-white donkey in the distance.

'Ha!' I cried, becoming literary again. 'Another wild jest of God! We search for the great white horse and all we get is a donkey. I ask you!'

I fell back into the seat and lit a cigarette, sadder than I'd been for a long time, because Mystras was a miracle, and they're hard to come by these days, and I knew I might never go back, horse or no horse.

It was late afternoon in the village; no one was out of doors except a very slight old fellow who had just emerged from the *café-neon*.

'Hello – you there!' cried the George, rolling down the window and beckoning for the man to come over. 'We've come a long way to Mystras and we have heard of a legend of a great white horse – the ghost of the emperor Constantine.'

'Yes, we have heard that his spirit still hovers over the city and has been known to appear in that form,' I said. 'Please tell us – do you know of such a legend?'

The old fellow leaned in the window and shook his head slowly. 'I've lived here all my life,' he said wearily. 'And I don't know what you're talking about.'

'Please don't go!' I cried. 'Maybe it's a secret, maybe you don't like talking about it. But you can tell us! *Was* Constantine ever seen on the mountainside in the shape of a great white horse? Is it true, is it?'

The man gave a dry cough, excused himself, and turned away. We heard him mutter a moment later: 'You *xeni!* You outsiders – you think of everything....'

Olympia
THE RUNNERS

I LEANED against the gate which led into the house of Phidias. Several glasses of the local wine, together with the local sun, had made me somewhat drowsy. I slid to the ground and rested, my back against the gate, in a fairly comfortable sitting position. The air was on fire. There were pine trees everywhere.

Nikos and I had come up that morning on a funny little slow train from Pyrgos. We'd passed the time watching the farmer in the front of the coach who was trying to keep track of his countless chickens and to haggle with the train conductor over the price of the ticket at the same time. Before he got off at his destination and disappeared in a cloud of feathers, he gave us several fresh eggs and an invaluable lesson on how to deal with train conductors. My vocabulary of Greek curses and insults was also vastly enriched from having listened to him.

About halfway to Olympia, I turned around and saw that two Gypsy women had settled themselves in the seats behind ours.

'Give me a cigarette,' one of them said, reaching out her hand. The Gypsies do not make a big thing of the word *please;* somehow, I like that.

'Give us another,' said the other.

The idea that it was their right simply to ask for what they desired was strangely refreshing. You needn't beg or plead; you merely state your case. Either you get the cigarette or you don't. You laugh, you cry, today is today.

Just as we were approaching Olympia, I turned around to have a word with them, and they were gone. I didn't recall the train having stopped since the time I gave them the cigarettes. I smiled to myself. I loved and envied those two perfume-laden, black-haired, wild-eyed ladies. I wished that I could move with their ease through a world of pure sunlight, a world as golden and seductive as the earrings they wore.

And disappear from a train that does not even stop.

Suddenly everything was green, and there were pine needles all over the place. The shops in the town were full of plates and egg-cups made from a pine wood so fragrant that you wouldn't dare eat from them. Blankets so gorgeous you wouldn't dare sleep with them. Shawls you wouldn't dare wear.

In the cafés, the inevitable countless cats waited under the tables for bits of *salata* or *souvlakia* or anything edible. Then we spotted a familiar-looking red polka-dotted kerchief; we tried to duck out of sight. Too late; they'd seen us. It was the insanely enthusiastic American couple we'd met the night before in Pyrgos. They had brought their car from New York and were Doing Greece, only they were having trouble finding it. The night before, they had completely lost Olympia, and when we had them they were less than an hour away from the place, they had almost died. Now here they were again, waving madly from the café for us to join them.

We cheerfully waved back, made like we were in a mad hurry, and continued on our way.

I had to see the Hermes of Praxiteles before I could even breathe, so we plunged into the museum and frantically wended our way to the special room where the Hermes is kept. I'd seen many photographs of the statue before, and read a number of descriptions of it — but nothing had prepared me for the total shock which I experienced in the inner room.

My previous conceptions of the male body went up in flame, smoke, or whatever. I saw the purest form of a man rejoicing in itself, totally at one with itself, almost sickeningly pleased with itself. The big toes drove me mad, until I got to the ankles, at which point I was on the verge of an epileptic fit. I proceeded to the calves, telling myself that I must take one day at a time. Wisely, I overlooked the knees, because I realized that I must save my strength for the thighs. Encountering the thighs, I gasped at the delicate veins insinuating their way through the marble flesh.

I walked slowly round and round, carefully avoiding the torso and its components. (The components are left to the reader, as they should be. Suffice it to say that they componed.) I proceeded to the ribs, then tried to ignore the shoulder-blades, which were exquisite wings.

His face is rather like the face of your younger brother, if you have one, or maybe your younger sister. Or maybe somebody you will meet tomorrow at a grape festival or a poetry reading.

I marvelled at the back of his knees — a part of the anatomy much overlooked by people and artists. They were the most interesting and sexy back-of-the-knees imaginable. There should be a special word for those two very private places in the body; maybe in some languages there is. A sculptor friend of mine has made up a word that sounds right: *knove*. Anyway, *knoves* are not present in the paintings on ancient Greek amphoras, where there is generally a baffling lack of communication between upper and lower arms, thighs and calves, almost as though the ancient figures move in a dimension where knees and elbows do not exist.

But how many 'dimensions' has the Hermes? Following the lines from the top down, I came to the conclusion that whereas the head bone is connected to the neck bone, and the neck bone to the shoulder bone, and the shoulder bone to the chest bone, and so on... the astoundingly beautiful muscles and sinews and subtle veins beneath the skin defy description. The statue seems to exist in another, nameless dimension of reality – perhaps in the 'space/time warp' or whatever we want to call it, where art reaches out to greet the Infinite. Where beauty exists on its own terms, and is intended to strike the beholder dead, or to force him to re-think what reality is all about, or at the very least – to make him weep.

It was time to leave, and do the arena. We took pictures of each other in front of the pedestal which has been used to light the Olympic flame since the time of the ancient games. Then we charged down the length of the arena, and invisible spectators must have cheered us on to victory, because we both won. We settled down on the grassy slope and amused ourselves by watching the two German tourists who were stripping down to shorts and T-shirts in preparation for their own race. One of their companions sounded the get-set-go, and the two young men bolted away from the starting line. I wondered where they were going. *To the other end and back, of course* – said my conscious, logical mind. *From here to eternity* – said another informing intelligence located farther back in my head. *They are racing back through time....*

'Here we are,' I said, leaning back against the cool grass, 'In the Year of Our Lord 1971, watching some Olympic games right here in Olympia!'

'After this, we should go to the temple of Zeus,' said Nikos.

'But we passed it, didn't we? All those fallen columns that look like gigantic slices of salami. All those French tourists peering into the dust with magnifying glasses. And what if we bump into those two American dingbats who drove across the Atlantic and got lost less than an hour from Olympia? I'll tell you what — let's go to the house of Phidias, the sculptor who created the giant Zeus, one of the wonders of the ancient world! It was so wonderful that it got stolen, and nobody knows where it ended up ...'

'I'd rather see the temple of Diana,' said Nikos.

'I don't want to see Diana — I want to see Phidias!' I cried.

'Well I want to do Diana!'

'OK. You do Diana and I'll do Phidias, and we'll meet in twenty minutes at Zeus.'

'All right, as long as you don't get into a long conversation with the guard, or start collecting hundreds of pine cones, like you did at Sparta.'

'OK. *Entaxi.*'

Strolling down the arena, we almost collided with the two German runners who were on their way back to the starting line. It was as though they had moved back in Time, and were now returning to the present. We didn't wait to find out who won. We left the arena and passed by the temple of Zeus again. *How awful to be Lord of the World,* I thought, *and to have all the columns in your temples fall down.* Then we went our separate ways — Nikos for Diana and me for Phidias. I don't know why I felt quite so strongly about seeing the ruins of the famous sculptor's house and studio. I felt a little silly about my stubbornness, silly and very, very drowsy. That's when I leaned against the gate, and slid down to a comfortable sitting position. The air was on fire, and the cicadas went on and on and on....

'Did Phidias ever sculpt Diana?' I heard myself asking out loud.

A voice very nearby promptly answered *No*. I turned around lazily, and saw the guard who was consulting a guide-book, and leaning against an olive tree. He looked like a cross between Jeff Chandler and Jack Palance. (This is because Chandler and Palance appeared in a film called *Sign of the Pagan*, back in the Fifties.)

'How do you know?' I asked.

'Know what?'

'That Phidias never sculpted Diana.'

'Because it is not written. Not written *here*,' he said, showing me the guide-book.

'Guide-books are not always right,' I said.

'So? Neither is the Bible.'

We gazed at the sun, which is not a wise thing to do in Olympia. Eventually, rubbing my eyes, I mentioned that I had a rendezvous shortly at the temple of Zeus.

'Forget Zeus!' said the guard. 'Come with me to Athens. The lights, the people, the cafés!'

'I've just come from Athens. All those tourists jumping into the fountain in Omonia Square. All those washrooms, which must date back to the early Byzantine period, where you stare at a hole in the floor and wonder what to do with it. All those steep streets where you take you life into your hands, especially if you're wearing slippery sandals. All those gorgeous dark-eyed men who strip you naked with a single glance. All that ice cream!'

'I *like* ice cream,' said the guard, somewhat defensively.

'So do I. But right now I want to find out what happened to the famous work of Phidias, the great statue of Zeus, stolen in times of yore and taken to God knows where.'

The guard consulted his guide-book. Trees swayed in the breeze. The fallen columns of the temple of Zeus just lay there. The amorphous interior of the house of Phidias grew more golden and hazy in the afternoon light. I began to wonder what it must have looked like when the great sculptor lived there. It was a smallish place, not much bigger than a bachelor apartment. There must have been many large jars full of olive oil and grain, and wine the colour of sunlight. He might have had concubines, maybe even a wife.

Everything was becoming gold. My hands, when I held them up to my eyes, were gold. The face of the guard was gold.

'How did Phidias sculpt the great statue of Zeus in gold?' I asked. 'It was gold, wasn't it?'

'Probably. At least partly. Anyway, you don't *sculpt* in metal, Miss. You make a model, you make a mould, then you *cast* in metal.'

'Oh.'

'And when is your rendezvous at the temple of Zeus?' asked the guard.

'Well ... as soon as I've finished here,' I said vaguely.

'Oh, and when do you think that will be? Do you think you'll ever be finished here?' he asked. His black eyes sparkled like pieces of onyx.

I began to realize that something was dreadfully wrong. For one thing, when I tried to get up, my limbs felt as though they were swimming in a sea of honey.

'Where... where do you think the ancient thieves took the great statue...?' I asked dreamily.

The guard started to laugh. He laughed and *laughed* and laughed. 'Where do you think?' he said. 'To that other nameless dimension of reality, of course! How did you put it? That "space/time warp" where art reaches out to greet the Infinite. Where beauty exists on its own terms, and is intended to strike the beholder dead...'

'...or force him to re-think what reality is all about,' I murmured. 'Or at the very least – to make him weep...'

'Precisely. And *that's* where they took the Zeus.'

'Do you really think so?' I asked, managing to look the guard in the eye.

'I know so,' he said. Then he leaned back again against the olive trees and listened to the cicadas.

I watched him for a long, long time. He was very beautiful, and he too belonged to another dimension of reality. Praxiteles and Phidias had laboured over just such beauty as this, wrenching it out of the neutral clay of the Now, the Present, and preparing it for its proper place in the eternal order of things. But their beauty had been static; his, I knew, would be defined in motion.

'Have you spent much time in the arena?' I asked.

'Yes,' he answered, with an odd sort of crooked smile. 'I never was an athlete, a runner... but I've spent a lot of time there...'

'You've been to a lot of places...' I said.

'Yes, I've spent a lot of time in a lot of places.'

When he turned to me, his face started to dissolve into pools of light. I noticed the clay on his hands. Now I knew what was happening.

'I fell asleep,' I explained when I got back to the temple of Zeus. 'I wasn't collecting pine cones or anything. I just fell asleep.'

A familiar red polka-dotted kerchief was bobbing along

through the pine trees; the American couple were on their way to the house of Phidias. The German runners, having returned to the starting point, had gotten dressed again and were now doing Diana. The Gypsies were nowhere and everywhere.

The Island

A DIARY

THE island is shy and exuberant, savage and fair, bold yet self-effacing. It is a woman in heat, a man in despair, a blonde horse at sunset, a riot of fig trees, a flaking white salt bed, an arid garden of thyme and oregano, a hundred clotheslines full of octopi hung up to dry, a warm night of fireflies and tiny shrimps with burning eyes.

You know you are almost there when you can see the two huge rocks they call 'the doors' rising from the sea ahead of you. The ship stops at a large island; from there, a motorboat takes you across the transparent green water to a smaller sister island. At the dock, the fishermen are spreading out their saffron yellow nets to dry, and women carrying large loaves of bread and plastic bags full of tomatoes and eggplants are laughing at some impossibly funny joke. Bare-footed boys with nutbrown bodies run along the beach chasing something only they can see, and in the café, the old men sip their afternoon coffee, play *tavali,* or simply smoke their pipes and watch the sea.

Suddenly you know that you have been here forever.

Entry One: We are staying in the tiny house where Nikos was born. It is really one room, with a stone floor and white stucco walls; it is very, very old, and it is joined to the row of similar houses which line the 'main street' of the village. It is lit by kerosene lamps — (electricity is still a relatively new convenience on the island) — and we fetch our water from an outdoor tap down the road, in the same kind of redbrown earthenware jugs that have been used for centuries in the East. They look strange, sitting on the windowsill along with the modern blue and yellow plastic ones. Stranger still are the faded family portraits of men with sailor's caps and large mustaches and women with their hair pulled back tightly into buns, who may have had their pictures taken only once in their lifetimes, and who stare in shy bewilderment from the dusty oval frames. Beside them on the wall are snappy colour photos of the younger generation all dressed up in miniskirts and tight pants smiling for the photographers in the cafés or nightclubs of Athens.

An incredibly old woman who used to be the village midwife has greeted us four times today, and asked us each time who we are and where we come from. She is more and more delighted each time we tell her, as though she can't get enough of the novelty of it all. She has an enormous wart on her chin, and she sits outside her door on a rickety old chair, her ancient body doubled over in an almost foetal position, chuckling softly to herself. 'Welcome, welcome!' she cries, each time she sees us. Perhaps tomorrow she'll remember our names, perhaps not. Her failing memory must mean that every day is utterly new to her — almost like being born again each morning.

About an hour ago she drew me close to her and said, 'If you go for *bagnio* (swim) in the sea, it is very good for your skin. It heals all your wounds. But you must take off your rings, or the sea will take them away. Yes, didn't you know? The sea *steals your gold*...! I don't know why, but this is true.'

Entry Two: I have met the mayor, the doctor, the school teacher, the man in charge of the post-office, telephone and telegraph system, and the chief of police of the island. I must try to remember their names and faces — (the mayor, I learned, was insulted when I failed to recognize and greet him an hour after we were introduced). The man in charge of the post-office, telephone and telegraph system, sits all day at his desk with earphones, scowling and listening to garbled messages coming from Athens or the surrounding islands, to which he responds with screams of ever-increasing frustration and even anger. He is intensely overworked. The chief of police, on the other hand, is a study in boredom. He has nothing whatever to do, due to the delightful fact that there is virtually no crime on the island, so he spends much of his time sitting in the café clicking his worry-beads, playing cards and waiting, helplessly, for something to happen. We have toyed with the idea of creating a crime for him to solve — something very Sherlockian, perhaps some sort of baffling theft. We would slip cryptic notes under his door, and plant outrageously meaningless clues all over the village. It would become know as The Case of the Six-Legged Octopus, although we still haven't figured out where the octopus comes in.

I also met a sad chap called Christos, whose melancholy, I learned, is due to the fact that he had refused to put his life savings in a bank; he kept the money, in paper, in a hole in the wall. When he went to look at it one day, it was all chewed up by mice. When he took the shreds to the banks, they refused *him.*

But most important of all, I have met Odysseus.

Odysseus has one leg, and baffling skyblue eyes, and when he smiles his shy wide smile, you can see that some of his back teeth are pure gold. He lives in a small room across the street from the church of Saint Nikolaus, and he doesn't like people very much, and that includes larger People like God and the Virgin Mary. He is the butt of a thousand jokes and rather cruel tricks, because he believes absolutely everything anyone tells him. Once someone told him that a beautiful young woman had come all the way from Tripoli to be his bride; he immediately made a journey to another island to buy fancy underwear for his betrothed. But there was no bride. Another time someone told him a queen was coming to see him; she was going to land on the northern side of the island in a helicopter. Odysseus got dressed up and waited, but there was no queen.

Sometimes he goes to the famous *spilio* – the great cave where, some say, the fabled Odysseus met the Cyclops. And there, he sells *gazoza* and orange drinks to the thirsty tourists who pour in to see the gigantic stalactites and marvel at the fabulous caverns. 'Look!' he exclaims, pointing to the boxes and boxes of empty pop bottles outside the cave. 'Look at all that work; I opened them all myself!'

His face, although lined now and weatherbeaten, still wears the clear, alarming expression of the eternal child. Someone once tried to warn him that the people were making a fool of him, but he smiled and shook his head and said that wasn't true, men couldn't be that cruel. Men were good, men didn't hurt each other. They only tried to have fun. He also tried to have fun, but he did it better alone. Sometime later he tried to hang himself on the bell-rope of the church for love of a village girl who could never be his.

'Why does he smile so much?' I asked Nikos. 'He can't have much to smile about.'

'He's just showing off his gold teeth,' Nikos said. 'He went to a dentist a few years ago and had some of his perfectly good teeth extracted so he could have them replaced with gold. The ancient Greeks, you know, used to carry coins in their mouths if they didn't have wallets, but that's beside the point. I just mean that he's literally got his life savings in his mouth. He's smarter than poor old Christos, when you come to think of it. The mice can't get at *that!'*

Odysseus, I love you.

Entry Three: The island is full of churches and shrines — some of them in the village and others nestled in the hills or higher up in the mountains, their domes like the perfect white breasts of the Mother. Each is devoted to a particular saint and the women leave *tama* — votive offerings — in the form of little metal plaques engraved with pictures of eyes or hands or feet, in the hope that the holy powers will intervene in the daily matters of health and safety. Sometimes there are sprigs of wild thyme or sweet basil hung by string or pink ribbon around the ikons. Sometimes there are lonely, dried-up flowers. Authentic Byzantine ikons hang side by side with modern plastic atrocities, and somehow it doesn't matter; holiness is holiness. When I came across boxes of detergents and dustcloths tucked in behind an ikon of the Virgin Mary, I remembered that the Greek word *katharos* means 'clean' or 'pure' both on the physical and spiritual level. Catharsis is a purification of the emotions, according to Webster, and that is holy. Every simple daily act performed with love is holy. I thought of all the women who tended these chapels through the centuries, down on their knees scrubbing the floors, the work itself an act of worship.

Today I went into the smallest and oldest chapel in the village, which dates back to the Thirteenth Century at least. It was pure white and empty, save for two ikons. Only a wooden partition, the *ikonostasis,* flanked by faded embroidered curtains separated me from the area of the Holy Altar, which is out of bounds to members of my sex. *God can get me if He wants,* I thought. *I'm going in anyway.* I proceeded to commit my act of *hubris.*

Behind the partition, in the sanctuary, the small altar was covered with a white cotton cloth. There was nothing else there — except, to my amazement, a flat wooden carving of Christ on the cross, propped up against one wall. It was so roughly done it might have been the work of a child. Curious, I turned it over. There were some letters stamped on the back. It was a piece of wood from a Coca-Cola crate.

I wanted to cry, which is nothing new because I do it all the time, and when I stepped out from the sanctuary my eyes were so watery that I didn't see the little lamp of holy oil which was hanging in front of me. I walked right into it, bashing my head against it, and winced with pain as the burning oil trickled into my hair. I thought I was dying; my scalp was seared with the heat, and I ran outside to find water, anything, to ease the agony.

My hair is still quite oily, even after several shampoos. But it's all right. God was not displeased because I invaded the *Holy of Holies.* On the contrary — I have been anointed.

Entry Four: The soft porous stone at one of the beaches is like a lung. When you lie on it, you can hear the sea breathing and wheezing as the waves enter the little sea-caves and force the air up through the holes in the stone. The beach is strewn with dry seaweed like shredded paper. We dove for little black sea-urchins, and ate about a dozen of them, prying them open with a knife, squirting them with lemon juice, and scooping them out of their shells. Then Nikos went down again and came back with an incredible shell creature called a *pina.* This has to be seen to be believed. It is about ten inches long and shaped rather like a thin fan tapering to a sharp point. It never goes anywhere; that is, it gets itself firmly embedded by its tip in the sand on the seafloor and simply stays there forever, waiting for various edible creatures to pass by. It is an incredibly silly and ignorant thing and has, literally, no mind of its own. In fact it can survive only with the aid of one or two tiny shrimps which live inside its shell and act as its brain. When anything that might be food for the *pina* comes floating or swimming by, the shrimp (or shrimps) go down to the tip of the shell where the meaty blob is situated, and tickle it. The blob is thus stimulated to action; the top of the shell opens and the food is trapped inside. Thus, a *pina* without a shrimp is a dead *pina*. It will simply sit there in the sand and starve to death, having nothing that can pass for a brain to inform it to open its shell from time to time. Nikos and I have thought up a new term to describe a witless person — a *pina* without a shrimp. That's a very *in* joke; it sounds better in Greek. But in all fairness to this odd creature, I should add that it's very beautiful when pried open; the inside of the shell is a dazzling world of phosphorescence, almost like mother-of-pearl. The blob tastes good too, with a dash of lemon juice and a little *ouzo*.

I was suffering from that bane which travellers the world over know by different names; here in Greece I suppose it would be 'Agamemnon's Revenge'. I looked around for a suitable place to squat; the landscape was utterly bare, and my only hope was a small prickly shrub at the top of a hill. I headed for it with the glazed stare of a person with one mission, and one mission only. A donkey, chewing thoughtfully on something in a field nearby, turned and stared at me as I relieved myself with a sigh. Indignant, I tried to outstare him; it was no use. There was only me and him, the sea and the urgent sun in all the universe.

Nikos and I went fishing off the rocks at the northwest tip of the island. The very best baits are the tiny shrimps which are found in the small pools in the hollows of the rocks, and to catch them you have to cup your hands in the water, remain perfectly still, and wait for them to come. It seems they are somehow fascinated with the colour of the human hand, and when you feel the first funny little tickle of their feet on your fingers you close your hands as quickly as possible and trap them.

Nikos caught interesting fish, but I got nothing except a large red particularly hideous sea-caterpillar. In fact I caught it three times; I kept throwing the abominable thing back into the sea and it kept taking the bait. By the third time, I think it was too exhausted to try again.

We dove again with masks and snorkels off the rocks. Underwater is a silent, magnified world of rippling light, and waving plants with feathery tentacles, and schools of white fish which gaze at you sideways with frightened eyes, then dart away like magic. I swam out once deeper than I should have; the rocks fell away, and before me was a chasm of terrifying electric blue. I am a good swimmer and I'm not afraid of deep water, but this was another kind of depth. It was utter mystery, timeless, bottomless as the soul itself. I hovered over it for a few moments — then, trembling, turned back towards the rocks. To the left of me something silver and triangular was undulating its way towards me. I clambered up onto the rocks screaming 'Shark! Shark!' Nikos immediately dove in, and came up a moment or two later, laughing, and holding up a small bag made of aluminum foil. Maybe poets should stay away from the sea, and —

> *Perhaps we are only dim figures underwater*
> *meeting for a moment*
> *the perfect eyes of fishes*
> *which encounter us sideways*
> *in luminous surprise*

And perhaps on land we hang on
to our illnesses which protect us
from the full responsibility of health

And perhaps on land we do not have
to answer for our crimes
while undersea we answer
and the sea will answer for itself

I had a conversation once with the underwater photographer, Ley Kenyon, who intrigued me when he said that there is really nothing to fear in the sea but oneself. Maybe then it was the self which confronted me in that bottomless blue chasm — (no other beast was lurking there). He had laughed when I suggested that we might all meet one day at Santorini — more properly called *Thera* — where archaeologists are carrying on underwater excavations and recovering relics of a civilization which, according to the Greek scholar Marinatos, was the fabled Atlantis. 'Don't you know how *deep* you have to go to find a single thing?' he exclaimed. And I wrote sometime later:

Drop the sails and be silent
There is something here we do not understand

As dark as the receding tides
As delicate as the tiny shrimps who
Tickle their way across my hands

There is nothing to fear in the sea
But ourselves
There is nothing to fear but man

A beautiful shell which I'd placed on a rock heaved itself over the edge in a kind of crazy suicide attempt, then began making its way back to the sea. I had forgotten that shells had live things inside of them; I had forgotten a lot of things. I was gaily swimming along close to the beach, imagining that I was Cousteau, when a shimmery, transparent jellyfish came floating along towards me. It was a bubble of living light; I had to have it. Nikos was jumping up and down and crying 'No, no!' just as I cupped my hand around the creature and received a devastating sting as it went poof and died on me, a deflated pool of slime. My hand burned for hours afterwards.

On the beach, Nikos was wrestling with the small octopus he'd just harpooned. It was coiled around his hand and wrist and halfway up his arm, hanging on for dear life. He pried it off and then proceeded to dash it many times against a flat rock. To anyone who hasn't seen this procedure it seems at first to be rather gruesome. On my first day on the island I'd seen a man far out on the rocks raising something in his hand and repeatedly smashing it on the ground; it looked almost like some sort of horrible murder. Actually, it's a very common sight on the island, and octopi are caught by the hundreds every day. The first smash against the stone ensures that the creature is dead, after which, repeated smashings force a grey-white soapy substance out of its body, in order that the meat will be tender enough to eat. If this is not done, octopus meat can be very tough indeed. After the octopi have turned from red to pale grey, they are hung up on lines to dry, and are barbecued or boiled later on. One of the things that bewilders visitors to the island is the sight of clotheslines full of dangling tentacles; it's a little disarming at first, and many people make faces and say *Ugh*. But I've come to regard it as an awfully beautiful sight.

By accident Nikos later harpooned a huge red starfish. We brought it up onto the beach, and when we removed the harpoon, one leg came off with it. I wanted to cry (which, as I have mentioned before, is nothing new) until Nikos assured me it would be all right. 'They grow new parts,' he said. 'Don't worry.' And then, to my utter amazement, the lovely creature slowly began to make its way back into the sea, leaving its leg behind it.

Just before we were packing up to leave for the day, I noticed what looked like an unusual brown speckled stone in the shallows. When I moved to touch it, it literally burst into life. It opened up two large frilled flaps, revealing tiny organs with an almost human shape, and began to swirl these flaps and rapidly propel itself away. It looked for all the world like a funny little dancer swirling her skirts around her. It left a trail of brilliant purple ink behind it, then, finding a safer place, wrapped itself up and pretended again to be a brown speckled stone. We still haven't figured out what it was, although an old sailor in the village said he thinks it might be one of the strange creatures that now and again the sea brings in from the northern coasts of Africa.

Entry Five: There's a legend among Greek seamen that if ever you see a gorgeous mermaid rising out of the water at the bow of your boat, you must take care as to how you address her, for she is the sister of Alexander the Great. She will be seeking news of her dead brother, and if you want to have fair weather, you must tell her that the great Alexander still lives and rules.

Our friend Odysseus wants above all to find himself a mermaid. Every day when we return to the village after swimming and fishing he asks us if we've found for him a real live *gorgona*. 'No,' we say, 'But maybe tomorrow.' 'Promises, promises,' he laughs, and hobbles away across the town square.

Entry Six: Today we spotted Nikos' uncle out in a rowboat looking for lobster, peering into a glass-bottomed barrel and scanning every inch of the seafloor. Behind him, manning the oars, was an extraordinary looking fellow who kept dropping the oars and flailing his arms around and talking to himself.

'It's Dionysus,' Nikos informed me. 'They call him *O Trellos* — the crazy one. He's all right, really. He just talks to invisible people a lot of the time.'

I learned that when Dionysus was a boy in school he was good in everything except mathematics. He had the delightful habit of carrying a non-existent 'one' over into the second line of addition. For example, if he had to add 10 and 10 and 10, he'd say: 'Zero plus zero plus zero equals zero. *Carry One.*' The answer would then be 40. That's how he dealt with the mathematics of his early years. No matter how many Nothings he added up, he always carried that positive digit into the second line of figures.

It was clear from the beginning that Dionysus had an alarming mind. His teachers tore their hair like characters in a Greek tragedy. They told him that if he didn't learn to count right, he'd end up as a lowly fisherman, et cetera. He said that his greatest aspiration in life was to end up as a lowly fisherman, et cetera, and besides, you just couldn't throw two Nothings together without ending up with a Something, and any fool could see that.

Every day when school got out, he'd go down to the pier and watch his father unravelling the tangled saffron nets that were his world, and listen to salty stories of the sea. No one is quite sure exactly when he went mad and started talking to his invisible people. But now he drinks a lot of *ouzo*, and sometimes dances in the street, but most of the time he rows the boat when Nikos' uncle goes lobster fishing.

As I watched them, the uncle, who had his head so far

down in the barrel that he couldn't hear Dionysus'
monologue, suddenly began pointing with one hand to a
particular spot in the water. He'd obviously spotted a lobster,
and didn't want to lose sight of it. Dionysus, misinterpreting
the gesture somehow, began rowing around in a series of
erratic circles, then for some reason, shot off in a straight
southerly direction.

'Jesus Christ,' I said. 'If your uncle doesn't take his head
out of that barrel, they're going to end up in Crete!'

At any rate, the lobster was lost, and Dionysus and the
uncle screamed at each other all the way back to the village.

Entry Seven: There is so much to record. *Places* overpower
me, especially places electric with history, or myth. There
have been times in the past when I've stood in front of, say,
the Great Pyramid at Giza, or in the (so-called) Room of the
Last Supper in Jerusalem, feeling so stunned that my mind
at the time was able only to record trivia, or worry over
immediate physical concerns. *Did I bring enough cigarettes,
I've lost my comb, my sandal strap's broken,* and so on.

But yesterday, a trip to the island of Delos, a kind of dream
journey. I walked down the avenue of the marble lions which
line the Sacred Way leading to the main temples. Delos,
where Zeus came in the form of a swan to seduce Leda.
Delos, where Apollo was born, where Light was born. I
moved through the ruins in an eerie fluid state of suspension
in time and space. There was a time when no one was allowed to get born or die here; pregnant women and very old
people could not set foot on the holy ground.

The heat and the light were dizzifying, and I thought *I
must not faint, I must not stop here.* This is Delos, an island
outside of human time. *Record the lions, record the stones,
keep walking.* This is Delos, where you're not allowed to get
born, or die....

Entry Eight: Every afternoon we drink coffee with the old priest of the village. Papa Stephanos is well over eighty, and totally blind. His son, who is the official *papas* of the island, intones the morning and evening prayers in the church of Saint Nikolaus – a duty he performs with a certain lack of flair – and Papa Stephanos only presides over the ceremonies on very special holy days, two or three times a year. When he was younger, Nikos remembers, he had a voice that sent chills down your spine when he performed the ancient litanies. Nikos reminds him of this, and he smiles and sighs and says, 'Ah, I was a voice in the wilderness ...' and goes on sipping his bitter coffee, his black-robed form casting a great shadow on the white wall of the café.

When he was young, the villagers say, he was uncommonly strong. On the joyous eve of Easter, it is customary in many Greek villages for the *papas* to pretend to hold the doors of the church closed at midnight, against the throngs of worshippers. The people then cry 'Open up, open up!' and heave their weight against the doors, which of course promptly give way. But apparently Papa Stephanos was so strong he must have had the very might of God on his side, for when he put his back to the doors, barricading them with his shoulders, the villagers had a devil of a time trying to get in!

This is no doubt a slight exaggeration, but in any case, everyone remembers that the doors always took rather longer than necessary to get opened when Papa Stephanos' weight was behind them. I find myself remembering a very pale and lacklustre young priest in Athens who had so little feeling for his calling that we once caught him trying to change a lightbulb in the middle of a particularly difficult Byzantine chant. I wonder what happens to *him* on the eve of *Paskha* ? I have a vision of him spreadeagled on the floor of the church, face downward, the people gleefully marching into the church over the door, which has fallen on his back.

This afternoon Papa Stephanos' daughter Maria called to us from the porch of the little house where she lives and looks after him. She was ironing tea-towels with an enormous black iron full of red-hot coals. 'You're coming to eat with us tonight!' she cried, and the tone of her voice informed us that this was a command, not merely an invitation.

The house is situated in what is knows as the *Castro*, the circular core of the village, which dates back to the Thirteenth Century and perhaps even earlier. Everything is spotlessly white, for the women paint the stairs with white lime, and even draw white lines around the stones which pave the narrow streets, as they have done for centuries in the Cyclades. The *Castro* is unbelievably small, neat, and somehow unreal — like a stage setting or a miniature model for a village, rather than, as it once was, an actual fortress.

We went to visit at nightfall. The beams on the ceiling of Papa Stephanos' house were painted a weird shade of watermelon pink, and the walls were covered with sheets of plastic with wild floral patterns. Maria cooked dinner in a kitchen the size of a cupboard, and afterwards we sat outside on the porch and listened as the sea heaved long weary sighs in the distance. We barbecued some octopi over burning coals, and some little blue crabs that we'd pried out of their crevices in the rocks by the shore, using flashlights and penknives. I was sorry, afterwards, for the way we'd blinded them and trapped them in their homes. Being a delicacy is an awful fate, really, and these creatures were very beautiful, some of them tiny as spiders in our hands. The salty smell of the smoke, combined with the scent of the countless flowers which grew all around the house, sent us all into a state of utter euphoria. When Maria passed around glasses of the local *ouzo* – which tastes rather like a combination of *pernod* and molten lava – we became witty, profound, joyful and downright silly. Papa Stephanos, the lamplight dancing in his sightless eyes, began to sing old village love songs, the kind the young men used to serenade their sweethearts with. His voice, although a little shaky, was wonderfully resonant, and he made even those sentimental old tunes sound like hymns.

Later, he started telling us hilarious stories from the old days about some of the people on the island, chuckling gleefully each time he thought of another one. It seems that Christos – the man who had his life savings chewed up by mice – had once, many years ago, borrowed a flashlight from a friend. It was the first time Christos had ever used a flashlight, the friend turned it on for him, and Christos used it for a few hours, then decided it was time to turn it out. After blowing on it a few times, he realized that was not the way to extinguish the thing. So he dunked it in water, took it out, and discovered that the hellish thing was still lit. He dunked again; still no luck. When he finally got up the courage to return the flashlight to his friend, it was two days later. It was still lit.

Maria was hanging over the side of the porch, limp with laughter, when he started telling us the story about Dionysus and the red eggs. At Easter, which is the holiest day of the year in the Greek Orthodox faith, the people bring out baskets of eggs dyed red, crack them and eat them as one of the traditional ceremonies of *Paskha.* 'Christos anesti,' they say to one another. 'Christ is risen.' Well one year, the day *before Paskha,* Dionysus was seen standing outside the church of Saint Nikolaus defiantly holding up two red eggs in either hand. He gave them a resounding crack, peeled off the red shells, and solemnly ate the eggs. Then he stepped forward and shouted into the open door of the church 'You see? It doesn't mean anything! This *Paskha*, it's nothing! It's all satanic propaganda!'

Then he did a little jig in the town square, and went home, talking to his invisible people all the way.

By the time Papa Stephanos got to the story of how the mother of Odysseus once tried to do away with herself, Nikos was choking with laughter, and I joined Maria and hung over the side of the porch, weakly trying to keep myself from collapsing in a heap on the ground. Odysseus' mother, a proud and rather handsome woman, had at one time been slighted or insulted by a young man in the village. She vowed in a loud voice so that all could hear, that she would do away with herself that same day. She chose death by drowning, since the sea was so close by, and she intended to walk straight into the water, never to return. Followed by a few of the village women, who screamed and moaned and tried to make her change her mind, she staunchly walked down to the beach. The women tore their hair and wept, until she did a rather strange thing. She sat down on the sand and slowly began to take off her shoes and stockings. That did it; the women broke up with laughter. 'You don't want to get your stockings wet!' they cried. 'You want to die, but you don't want to ruin your shoes!' Burning with shame, but no doubt inwardly pleased and relieved, she gathered up her things and ran back to the village, convinced that life was the best thing after all.

Papa Stephanos wiped a tear from his eye, and I realized that it wasn't there from all the laughter, but rather from a great and boundless love for the people of his island. And I suspect that he was beginning to feel — as we all did — a little ashamed of ourselves for laughing so heartily at the foibles of others. If anyone could have seen us as we were that night, it would have been evident that *we* were the village fools.

It was getting late. We'd finished the last of the octopus and the *ouzo*, and Papa Stephanos looked suddenly very weary. We said goodnight. A shy, uncertain wind was feeling its way through the dry shrubs and crumbling stones of the *Castro*, as though in search of something lost centuries ago. Fireflies flitted here and there like bright particles of laughter. We went down to the harbour and leaned over the dock, shining a flashlight into the water to see the hundreds of tiny shrimps with burning golden eyes gazing up at us from the black depths.

In great laughter there is great love, I thought. And maybe being holy means being almost unbearably human. Papa Stephanos, I concluded, is a holy man.

The moon, the blind eye of night, cast silver benedictions on the water.

Entry Nine: We spent a post-rain morning climbing the drenched mountain-slopes in search of food for dinner. The electric storm of the night before had turned the village into a network of fabulous multi-coloured rivers, and the first light of dawn revealed dozens of fat grey-green snails. I had overcome my horror of these tender creatures since I first encountered them at Mystras. They were everywhere, sauntering forth from their crevices in the rocks in search of their moist and mysterious *petits déjeuners*.

The mountains were rampant with goats all sharing some secret joke, the way goats do — and we plunged upwards (if that is possible) into another world. We caught fifteen giant snails in ten minutes, and stuffed them into our knapsacks with some wild mint and thyme to keep them occupied. Then we lunched on boiled eggs and orange juice in the shadow of a small church, and tried to read an inscription in ancient Greek on a marble stone. It's terrible trying to read ancient Greek, especially when there's no space between the words. I mean: *itsterribletryingtoreadancientgreekespecially whentheresnospacebetweenthewords.*

Noon came darkly; more rain was afoot. We slid back down to the village and proceeded to set things up in order to cook what be believed would be a fantastic feast. So far so good. We lit the two oil-lamps in our tiny medieval home, and discussed our menu. *Escargots,* of course — (everything sounds delicious in French) — with a salad. Hollandaise sauce? Certainly! No problem — we'd whip it all up in a flash.

We had all the necessary ingredients: lettuce, tomatoes, mayonnaise, olive oil, lemons, and Whatever, all stuffed in multi-coloured plastic bags, which were lined up, row on row, in the storm-dark kitchen.

I said:

— *Okay, you do the snails, and I'll do the salad, right?*

— *Right!*

Shivering with excitement, we set about our task. It was about one-thirty in the afternoon. The village was asleep, because the villagers were wise. We were not wise; we were trapped in the strange ecstacy of French gourmet cooking on a Greek island in the Aegean sea in the middle of what might be a typhoon.

We put one lamp in the kitchen area, and one in the centre of the room where there was a table to work on the salad.

— *Oh no, there's no water,* said Nikos.

— *Damn,* I said, *I forgot to got down to the well. I'll go now*

So I took three plastic buckets — a red one, a blue one and a yellow one, and charged through the streets in my green plastic sandals to get water. Three different kinds of water - one for drinking, one for cooking, and one for Whatever. Five minutes later I was back, and Nikos had emptied our knapsacks of snails into a large iron pot. They squirmed and protested a little, but it was hard to tell because the light was so dim. We lit the gas stove, poured in water from bucket A, added salt and wild thyme, and waited.

— *I think I'll start on the salad now,* I said, gathering up tomatoes, mayonnaise, lemons, etc. into a white plastic bowl. I took them to the table and realized I had no knife.

— *Bring me a knife, please ...*

— *I can't. I'm using it for the garlic for the butter sauce ...*

— *Well clean the other knife from the cupboard with the water in the yellow bucket ...*

— *I can't see the yellow bucket. Bring me an extra lamp.*

— *I can't bring an extra lamp, or I can't see anything here.*

— *Well there's a hunting knife in my jacket pocket.*

— *I can't see your jacket pocket unless I have more light.*

The snails were boiling happily in the dark pot. I thought that if I could find my way to Bucket B, the blue one, I could use the fresh water from there to clean the extra knife which was in the cupboard. Of course, this meant that the water in Bucket B would become cleaning water instead of Drinking or Cooking Water. But that was OK, because then the contents of Buckets B and C would be used for Whatever, while the contents of Bucket A would still be cookable. On the other hand, it was rather difficult to make out the colours in the darkness.

— *If you give me a spare candle,* I said, *I can find the other knife and clean it.*

Nikos handed me a candle from the gloom of the kitchen.

— *Take care,* he said. *I accidentally used Bucket B to clean my hands, and that means that it smells of garlic.*

I thought that would be all right, because there's nothing wrong with a bit of garlic in a normal Hollandaise sauce. However, after I had found the extra knife, I realized that the lamp in the other room needed extra fuel, and I had to return to my salad with a dripping candle in one hand and a plastic container of oil in the other. I stood there, staring at the tomatoes and mayonnaise, paralyzed.

— *Nikos*, I asked feebly, *how are the escargots coming along?*

— *Great! Just smell that fresh thyme!*

By now, the atmosphere was a grey-green cloud of lamp oil, cigarette fumes, steam, boiling spices, all lit up now and again by a dramatic flash of lightning.

— *Do you have a spoon?* I cried, in mounting despair. *I don't think I can stir the Hollandaise sauce without one.*

— *Yes, I've got a spoon, but I used it for mixing the garlic and butter, so I put it in the blue bucket. Then I realized that I had to use the red bucket because that was cleaner.*

— *What about dishes?* I cried, casually tossing the salad with a penknife and my naked forefinger.

— *Over with the salt, in the corner.*

— *If I can borrow your lamp I can get to the corner.*

— *You can't borrow my lamp, or I can't watch the snails!*

I thought that if I could find my way to where the napkins were, everything would be solved, because then I could clean everything with napkins, even in the dark.

— *I'm sorry*, Nikos said. *I had to use the napkins to dry the spoon which was in the red bucket so you could stir the sauce for the salad. But now that you've already done it with the penknife, I used the spoon to stuff the cooked snails in their shells with the garlic and butter. Oh, do you have a light? The stove's gone off again.*

Lightning struck, and the rain poured down. It was Eden all over again. It was funny, it was Friday, it was everything. We dined on *escargots* and salade à la Hollandaise, and as we spoke, all the other snails in the mountains wagged their damned silly silent tongues. The goats held onto their hilarious secrets. It was the end of summer.

Entry Ten: The pine groves buzz with hornets. A slim white horse stands motionless in a field fuzzy with sunlight, like a creature out of Eden. A newborn calf, all wet and scared and funny, begins to examine the world on its shaky, spindly legs. Faces of little cats peer out from among the flowers. A magnificent young bull, pure white, is being run through the village to the slaughterhouse, followed by a tractor and half of the village kids who scream and laugh. Its eyes are wild as it crashes through the narrow streets. The eyes of ancient beasts must have looked like this when they were led to the sacrificial altars of the gods. A naked, bloody young lamb hangs upside down in the window of the meat store, a sprig of parsley in its mouth.

Laughing boys race through the village square on mules; they urge them on by striking them with chains around their cheeks and eyes. I do not like this. Down the road, the man who raises rabbits chooses one for some family's dinner. The red-eyed bunny stares, the cold steel of the knife at its throat, its whole body suspended by the ears.

We take two donkeys and go out for the day into the mountains and down into a beautiful plain at the southern part of the island. We find purple grapes and give some to the donkeys who chew them thoughtfully, the sweet juice dribbling down their chins. We visit many small churches, and then head down again to the coast. The wind is rising and the waves are frilled with white froth; there was talk yesterday of a *fortuna* coming — a great storm. But it will not hit full force until evening. Meanwhile nothing is happening, everything is happening. The donkeys know their way back home.

Entry Eleven: During the war, Nikos tells me, when the Fascists occupied the island, the kids used to steal potato peels from the garbage cans behind the houses where the German soldiers stayed, and roast them over little fires by night. Nothing was real in those terrible times except death, and hunger. Papa Stephanos used to scrounge up food, moving, like God, in mysterious ways, and distribute it among the poorest families in the village. No one is quite sure how he managed this — (I must remember to ask him some time) — but he probably went around to the larger farms which would have had some extra produce, even in wartime, and convinced the farmers to consider their own immortal souls and their fellow man.

After the war, someone opened a washroom in a small café which had been closed for years, and found it full of cockroaches and useless German marks. In the end, then, the paper money of the Third Reich had served only one, fitting, scatalogical purpose.

Entry Twelve: This morning, three black-robed sisters, girls in their early teens, walked arm in arm down the road to the church of Saint Nikolaus to attend the funeral of their father. It seemed that half of the village was assembled in the square outside of the church. As the girls approached, the crowd parted to let them through, and all the women began to sway and moan, their voices rising and falling in eerie cadences, in the ancient, timeless music of mourning. The girls themselves looked like figures from a chorus in a Greek tragedy; their sobbing and wailing was totally unrestrained, and for a moment I felt that the scene was so pure, so perfect, it might have been rehearsed. That was my Western mind at work again; I was reared in a society which teaches children to hide their emotions, to keep a stiff upper lip, even if it means a lifetime of repressions and neuroses as a result. In the East there is no such thing as purely private sorrow. You let it all hang out — birth, life, death, everything. If necessary, you overplay emotions; you do not understate, you do not conceal. It is the only way.

In Greece, the dead are buried in the ground ... but after a number of years, there is a ceremony in which the bones of the dead are dug up and removed to the local church, where they are placed in enclosures in the walls, and marked by stone plaques. When Nikos told me that as a young child, he was present when they took his father's bones from the ground, I was stunned to think that children were allowed to witness such a (to my mind) gruesome procedure. 'But why not?' he exclaimed. 'Death is death, bones are bones. It serves no purpose to pretend otherwise.'

What I shall always remember about this place is its purity, its innocence, its open-eyed acceptance of the absolutes of life and death, darkness and light. And in some inexplicable way, here on this tiny Aegean island, I am coming to understand that light itself is the final mystery.

Entry Thirteen: Last night two of the villagers got into an unpleasant argument in the café. One of them spoke loosely of the other's sister, and, this being tantamount to a declaration of war, the insulted party called in the mayor as witness to the slander. Plans were immediately made for court proceedings. This morning, despite very treacherous weather, the two men left the island in separate boats, keeping a wide and angry distance between one another. The mayor and his secretary accompanied the insulted party. This would be a simple story except for one thing: the island where they must take their case to court is relatively close to here. But because no boats go there directly from this island, they have to go to a neighbouring island where they'll board a large boat for Piraeus on the mainland — (a journey of some six hours) — and from *there* make their way back to where they'll appear in court. If they had a helicopter, they could be there in twenty minutes; it's a shame. But on the other hand, as someone said a short while ago, going by this huge and ridiculous circular route, any one of three things might befall them. They could die of boredom; they could make amends and play *tavali* all the way back, or they could be shipwrecked, because another big storm is on the way. In any case, a principle is a principle.

Entry Fourteen: It's *ouzo*-making time on the island. Every October, some time after the grapes have been harvested and shipped off to outside markets, and after the island has made its own wine, it's time to distill the quintessential brew which I earlier described as a combination of *pernod* and molten lava.

Whatever's left over from the grapes which were pressed for wine — skins, seeds, leaves and twigs — is stored underground for a few weeks. Then it becomes a fermented purple mass which is dug up and shovelled into huge cauldrons heated by wood fires. Through a series of ducts and pipes the potent vapour travels, is distilled, until finally the fire-water emerges, drop by drop from a faucet, and is collected in buckets. The work goes on day and night; there must be a least two men doing shifts to keep everything moving. I don't know how much *ouzo* is produced at the end of all this, but it's probably quite enough to supply the island for a year.

Tonight Nikos and I went to the little shed which is the local distillery to watch the proceedings. As we approached, the air was burning with the pungent aromas of what seemed to be the product of some medieval alchemy. Inside, the heat was overpowering, and in the glow from the fire, the faces of the workers were red and gold. The chap who was changing the buckets laughed at our bewilderment, and he handed us a small sample of the *ouzo* to taste. He is one of the few older men on the island who is minus one arm — (there was a time when the fisherman used dynamite for fishing, and there were some unfortunate accidents as a result). He laughed even harder when he saw the expressions on our faces after we'd tasted the brew. 'A little strong, eh?' he shouted over the roar of the fire. 'That's because it's the first bit to come from the tap. It's always like that.'

We learned that they do of course gauge the alcoholic content of the *ouzo*, and it's not bottled for consumption unless it is at an acceptable level. We left soon, laughing and gasping a little, our throats on fire.

We finally ended up at *Spiros' Club* which is close to the sea on the western side of the island, just behind the village. Mercifully, it being October, all but a handful of the summer tourists have left. There is a young gay Frenchman who's rented a room in the village and who's been here since June, an elderly German couple, two globe-trotting girls from South Africa, and ourselves, as the only *xeni* on the island. Spiros has made himself a mint this summer serving *retsina*, salads and fish and octopi to the tourists, and now he's a very happy man. The club is small; the tables are covered with plastic cloths in garish colours; the walls are adorned with faded reproductions of El Greco paintings; in the corner there is a huge, ancient juke-box with a repertoire which includes everything from Tom Jones to the latest Greek hits from Athens. Outside there is a garden where people can dance; it is enclosed by walls of tall swaying reeds and there is a large palm tree in the middle.

Spiros is going to close the place tomorrow, because we will be leaving. This makes him sad. He puts some coins into the juke-box, and we hear *O Sole Mio*, followed by *Lay Lady Lay*. 'Where is everybody!' he cries, and at that moment the police chief walks in with his friend Yannis. Yannis can dive deeper than anyone on the island and claims he can hold his breath underwater almost as long as a dolphin or a whale. He is also the best dancer on the island, and superb show-off. He was always dancing, I hear, — even as a child.

The Greeks have a dance called the *zembekiko*. It is normally performed by a male dancer who is either at the end or the beginning of his wits. Although one must adhere at all times to the strict and complex rhythm of the music, one is allowed all sorts of intricate variations, depending on one's ability and state of mind. The wisest time to attempt a *zembekiko* is when you are either totally sober or superbly drunk. Otherwise, the results may be disastrous, since you are likely to whirl like a dervish off the stage or swoon like a dying eagle in free fall. The dance is both a fight against gravity and a kind of flirtation with the earth. This should explain the following poem. Or perhaps the poem will explain the explanation, I'm not sure.

Greeks have two ways of talking
— face to face or side to side —
One speaks and the other watches
The nearest wall
Where the birth of other worlds
Takes place before his eyes.

The imperial and impermanent eagle
of the Byzantines
Had two heads that looked East and West
And tried to gather God
Into a single body
— the body of a bird —

I spoke before of a will that flirts
With eagles, and now I speak
Of eagles who flirt with earth
In their wide slow turning,
Their descent, their dialogue with death.

Then poised on some craggy cliff
Of mountain or of mind, they wait
For the updraft, breath of God, pure wind
To hoist them into heaven once again.

Whether with broken or unfailing wings
They fly, they rise, they fall

So with these dancers on the broken edge of midnight
Born with the sign of the double-headed eagle,
Dancing still.

After some unnecessary prompting, Yannis gets up to dance. He puts a sprig of basil behind his ear and waits to hear the first hypnotic notes of the *bouzouki* playing the long, maddeningly seductive prologue to the *zembekiko*. He concentrates, spreads out his arms, walks around in slow figure eights, deliberately tantalizing us. He drops his cigarette on the floor, grinds it out with his foot — (never losing a single beat of the music) — and then, using the cigarette as a focal point, staring at it scornfully, he begins to dance complex, provocative circles around it.

The music quickens; Yannis crouches down and gives the floor a resounding spank with his open palm. Then suddenly he leaps up into the air, an uncoiled spring, demanding the right to fly. He drops again, touching the floor reverently with the back of his hand, brushing it, caressing it. He swivels on his heels back and forth, his head turning, addressing the four corners of the earth. His face has taken on the radiance of a child. He laughs and snaps his fingers, he whistles wildly and hisses between his teeth. His expression tells us that the world begins and ends here, that there is nothing on earth right now to compete in importance with this joyous celebration of the body, this study in fury, this mind-bending, defiant dance.

He's got it now; he's one with the dance; he *is* the dance. He's animal and bird, water and fire – he is a man free of the earth yet one with the earth, his body exploring the frightening dual nature of freedom.

'*Ellah*, Yannaki, *ellah!*' we cry. 'Come on!'

He conducts the invisible orchestra in the juke-box. He does a forward somersault, landing at the bottom of a chair which he then proceeds to pick up in his teeth, balancing the weight against his chest. His feet have not once lost the rhythm of the dance. He puts the chair down, and with a few more leaps and controlled, crashing falls, concludes the performance. We clap and pound the tables in appreciation, sending a few black olives rolling onto the floor. From here on in, the evening is made. We eat enormous amounts of fish and cheese, drink amber *retsina*, and feed the insatiable juke-box until we're down to our last few *drachmas*.

Spiros is almost in tears when we decide we must go. It has been a wonderful summer for him; it's over now. The gay young Frenchman who shyly shared our table and said little, slips out into the garden. Just as we are leaving, we see him by the palm tree with an invisible partner in his arms, waltzing to the strains of *O how we danced on the night we were wed....*

The music follows us all the way down the dark path back to the village.

Entry Fifteen: I pack up the odd assortment of things that we will take away with us: a giant sponge, a crucifix made of tiny shells, eleven small beige starfish, a piece of wood which the sea caressed and then rejected, a tea-towel from Maria embroidered with Byzantine crosses, a bunch of wild mountain thyme, a rusty goat's bell, a beeswax candle from the church of Saint Nikolaus ...

Odysseus is standing by the old gnarled eucalyptus tree in the village square, his cap tilted at a cocky angle, his blue eyes watching us. He smiles, and his smile is shot with gold. 'Good weather for sailing!' he says, 'But of course, one never knows ... How far is Canada? Maybe I'll come one day. Is it farther than Gibraltar? I've been to Gibraltar. Goodbye, goodbye....' We shake hands, and make our way down to the harbour.

Papa Stephanos is sitting in his usual chair outside the café — an eternal figure in black against the dazzling white wall. I think: *he will be here forever, he will never die.* We lean over to kiss him; there are tears in his eyes. 'Come in the spring!' he says. 'We will go to the mountains to celebrate *Paskha* ... we will all go together ...' We leave him sipping his bitter coffee, his hands trembling a little as he raises the cup to his lips. 'Goodbye, children, goodbye....'

Farther on down the road, Nikos' aunt emerges from her house, carrying a large pink plastic bag. 'Here, take this. Food. It's a long trip to Athens. There's some boiled eggs and tomatoes and cheese and bread....' She bursts into tears and crushes us in her ample arms. '*Kalo taxidhi!* Have a good journey!'

By the time we reach the harbour, many laughing children have gathered behind us, their voices like little bells in the clear vibrant air. The motorboat is waiting; we jump in and wave to everyone on the dock as we speed away. The island gets smaller and smaller. It is as though we are not leaving it at all — it is leaving *us.*

Later we board the big boat for the six hour trip north to Piraeus. I sit in a deck chair and watch the waves churning as we pull away towards the open sea. I remember the old sailor's warning: *'If you see a gorgeous mermaid rising out of the water, a gorgeous mermaid seeking news of her dead brother, say to her that the Great One lives yet, lives and rules. Say this if you want fair weather. She is the sister of Alexander.'*

I want to write a letter to Odysseus, a letter which I will send from Canada, which is farther than Gibraltar, a letter which goes:

Dear Odysseus:

I will send you a golden toothbrush and a real live mermaid, if you will send me a box of fireflies and tiny shrimps with burning eyes.

Yours truly, Gwendolyn.

Stones and Angels
A RETURN TO ATHENS

I AM back again in Christina's living room amid the mad clicking of the knitting needles. Five years have passed since I was last here, and only a very few things have changed. The kitchen and bathroom are full of birds in brightly decorated cages; the children have grown up and are listening to Cat Stevens and Pink Floyd in the bedroom. Irini has changed her hair colour, and Sophia has lost some weight. Someone has embroidered the Acropolis in green and yellow on a cushion cover. A new electric kettle screams for help in the kitchen.

Dina is one of those Athenians who has never been up to the Acropolis. ('You can see it from the window every day; it's just *there.*') With a fiendish gleam in her eye, she hands me two huge needles and a hefty ball of bright red wool. '*Knit,*' she commands as I look at her helplessly. '*Knit, knit!*' she cries, and I wither under her gaze. I begin the first line. The first line is always the hardest. I decide I will knit an epilogue of sorts, an afterword, a random pattern of thought since my return to Athens.

The city is getting tired; it is running on centuries of accumulated nervous energy and refuses to relax. And the city is scared as well. A few short years ago it tasted blood again in the nightmarish episode at the Polytechnical School when army tanks bore down upon the ranks of protesting students, killing and wounding in hideous numbers. The city is shaky, like someone recovering from a severe bout of flu, spending its energy in fitful bursts of activitiy, then lapsing into exhaustion. If anything, the pace of life is even more frenetic than I remember; the people seem to be unbearably impatient with the awkward, twitching realities of the times. They drum their fingernails, so to speak, in despair over the inadequacy of the present moment, tensely waiting for something, anything to happen which will provide a temporary escape from that moment.

Reality is not of the here and now, nor is it to be found in the past. Reality is the ever-elusive Something which is always one step ahead of you in time. It is one minute from now, one hour from now, and you must chase it; you must speed up time in an attempt to catch up with it. The slightest incident can send people into a flurry of talk or activity which quickly reaches a peak, then painfully ebbs as the waiting begins again. The waiting is a study in tension; it is almost the opposite of boredom. It is a kind of exhausting alertness, a spiritual insomnia which allows nothing to slip by the attention.

In Christina's living room, the women's voices rise and fall in theatrical cadences. Everyone butts in on everyone else, each trying to outdo the other in intensity of expression or sheer wordiness. Greek is a polysyllabic language; thus it takes *longer* to get something said, to make a point. North Americans are often convinced that because of all the dramatic facial expressions, gesticulations, and near-hysterical tones of voice, something of earth-shattering significance must be under discussion. Not always so, of course. It just looks and sounds that way to us Westerners with our language of monosyllables and monotones. When we want to stress or punctuate a point while speaking, often the best we can do is to wave a hand limply or raise a forefinger. Whenever possible, we understate, we 'play down', since it is of the essence for us in our society to keep our cool (whatever that is). The Greeks on the whole, and Athenians in particular, are not terribly interested in cool. Small wonder. Wagons of war, knights in dusty armour, horses, chariots,and now, tanks, have kept the fires of anger and passion raging.

Five years ago it was difficult to get from point A to point B in the city. Now, it is often impossible. The buses are slow, bulging caterpillars, and once one has squeezed, pushed and elbowed one's way inside, there is the awful prospect of having to get off. Most of the streets are too narrow to comfortably accommodate cars — (Athens was not built with the Twentieth Century in mind) — and taxi drivers all seem to be in varying stages of nervous breakdowns. The paraphernalia of worry-beads, small plastic pictures of saints, crucifixes and family photos which decorate the dashboards is powerless in working any kind of magic in traffic. The language of taxi drivers is their most eloquent defense, — a series of rapidly-fired curses, insults and soul-destroying anathemas hurled at pedestrians and other drivers alike, carefully constructed to deflate the bravest of the brave.

A few days ago I watched a film starring Greece's finest comedian, Thanassis Vengos. He is a genius of the comic art, and watching him, one is torn — as with all fine comedy — between laughter and tears. He is so utterly human, it is almost heartbreaking. He charges and surges across the stage or screen with blinding speed. He seems to be moving in all directions at once, and like a prism throws off beams of light and energy. He never walks; he jumps, runs and darts around continually, his face registering a kaleidoscope of emotions. The frenzy of movement never lets up, and if there is a gap in the action, he grabs anything within reach which is edible or drinkable and chews or gulps it down. He seems to be crashing through time in pursuit of some obscure and ever-changing goal, and he's a winner even when he loses. The Greeks adore him. In some ways he is the quintessence of the modern Athenian.

Christina brings in some tea, and the sound of Bob Dylan's *The Times They Are A'Changin'* comes pouring in from the bedroom.

'What kind of music is that?' exclaims Sophia.

A heated discussion follows, all about The Young People Of Today. I have the definite and uncomfortable feeling that I've been here before. One woman begins passionately to complain that her son is thinking of leaving Greece to go and study in some foreign land. Everyone is horrified; this is the most unthinkable of all the unthinkables. The Greek family is an extremely tightly-knit unit; the women are highly possessive with their children, and 'leaving home' is just not part of the established order of things. Even when young people go out to work and get married, the new family thus created becomes an appendage of the old one, and there is no transitional stage wherein one might get one's bearings, explore independence, examine the self.

'Why does he want to go?' she cries. '*Why?*'

'He probably doesn't want to go into the army,' I say. 'He probably doesn't want to learn how to kill.'

'So he'll go and join those long-haired students who shout and carry signs through the streets!' she exclaims, almost on the verge of tears. 'Look what happened to them! Look what they did to them!'

The women fall silent. Everyone is remembering. It was the 17th of November, 1973....

Students of the Polytechnical School in the centre of

Athens staged a demonstration to protest the fascist activities of the Greek government. The colonels responsible for the military *coup* of 1967 were still in power. The *Junta* government had sent thousands of Greece's finest artists, writers, and revolutionaries into exile and imprisonment — along with countless numbers of people who were simply known to have left-wing tendencies. The composer Mikis Theodrakis, whose music was used in the film 'Z', was one of the names at the top of the *Junta*'s black list. While in prison, he continued to write music, tapping out the rhythms on the bars of his cell and smuggling the work to someone on the outside. I met him once in Toronto; he's a great mountain of a man with wild hair and piercing eyes. He is gentle and soft spoken, but when he is conducting an orchestra he is a human dynamo; his arms become wings, and he looks as though he is taking part in the creation of the world.

Another name at the top of the list was that of the great poet Yannis Ritsos. The best, the very best of men were the first to be seized in that ugly year of 1967.

Then, six years later, the students of the Polytechnical School demanded that their voice be heard. It was the voice of the Greek people too long committed to silence. They gathered in the school and began broadcasting appeals to the people to rise up against their oppressors, through loudspeakers and over the radio. Military units gathered on top of the Hotel Acropolis across the street; guns were trained on the school day and night, but the students held their ground. Then, on November 17, the tanks moved in, crushing the iron gates of the school into grotesque, tortuous shapes. 'Stop! We are your *brothers!*' some of the students cried, waving their arms in front of the tanks. Then the shots rang out, and the bodies began to fall. Many were killed, many more wounded. It was a triumph of pure evil.

Now the years of the *Junta* are over, and the climate of

Greece, though somewhat safer, is still uncertain. The Polytechnical School stands as a grim reminder of the nightmare
of November 17th, 1973. The walls of the building are covered with revolutionary symbols, slogans, the names of the
dead, in many colours, the brightest of which is black. When
I passed the school a few days ago, the very air seemed to
change, become electrically charged. It is impossible, I think,
to pass by the place without having the feeling that something has *happened* there, even if one is unaware of the
actual story. Now the school has become a central meeting
place for the young, the politically conscious generation of
Greece. Talks, concerts and films are frequently held there,
and the day I passed, a new work by Theodrakis came
through the loudspeaker, filling the streets for blocks around
with the stunning music of human freedom.

That same night, Nikos and I went to visit the poet Yannis
Ritsos. We had done some translations of his poetry and,
needless to say, we were excited and somewhat nervous at
the prospect of meeting the man whom Louis Aragon once
called 'the greatest living European poet'. As we stood
waiting for the door to open, I remembered Ritsos' short
poem, *Obligation:*

A star shines in late evening like a lighted
        keyhole;
you press your eye to it — you peer inside — you see everything.
The world is shot full of light behind the closed door.

You've got to open it.

Yannis Ritsos greeted us at the door with open arms.
'You've come! Welcome, welcome!' he said, planting neat

kisses on our cheeks and leading us into his tiny, crowded apartment. It took me a moment to get my bearings. I knew, of course, that Ritsos is well-known for the drawings he creates on the natural surfaces of stones, bones and roots, and I had seen some photographs of these works, but nothing had prepared me for the sight which met my eyes. Floors, tables, shelves and mantelpieces were covered with an astonishing number of creations. Human figures sang from the stones, leapt from the tangled roots, crept out of the bits of bone in a stunning and bewildering variety of postures and expressions.

He smiled at our amazement and gave us a short guided tour of the rooms, stopping now and then to pick up a piece and comment on its origin, turning it over fondly in his hands. In every case, the face or figure was something which had been *discovered* within the natural contours of the material, never imposed upon it.

We sat in the living room and he brought some wine and candied fruit in tiny glass dishes. His movements had the slow and studied grace of one who has learned to respect time. Although he was sixty-seven, nothing about him would suggest he was much over fifty. His face, with its wonderfully regular, handsome features, bespoke great kindness and patience; his hazel eyes were keenly attentive, reflecting the gentle humour that only comes after much suffering. When he spoke, it was as though each word was a gift, a discovery, something to be handled with care.

'My work keeps me alive,' he told us. 'In creating, I am affirming my place in the universe, I am making a statement against death....'

Again and again in our conversation that evening, the subject of death arose. For Ritsos, it is not a morbid preoccupation but an ever-present reminder of the conditions of our mortality, a perpetual *why* that spurs us on to noble and beautiful endeavours, to a magnificent defiance. He was putting the finishing touches on a long poem written some years ago, a poem for Pablo Neruda, whose death saddened him deeply, whose life and work had so much in common with his own. He showed us the manuscript, painstakingly executed – as is everything he writes – in a beautiful calligraphy. He spoke of Pablo's struggles, and of his own; when he came to speak of his last 'detention' in the political prison on the island of Leros, it was without bitterness, only weariness and great sorrow.

He wrote his poem, *News Report*, in 1969:

Evening clouds; the lighted clock in the church in the square;
bald trees; cold; garbage. From the hilltops
gunfire could still be heard. A while later
George arrived on a bicycle. He laid down
a guitar with broken strings. He said
'We hauled the dead into a storeroom. No time for prayers or flags.
But hide this list at least, so in future we'll remember
their names, their ages – I've even got the measurements
     of their legs.
The three marble-workers were killed too. All that's left
is that stone angel, without a head – you can put any head
you like on it.' With that he left. He didn't take the guitar.

But despite the bleakness of these lines, his work is essentially affirmative; it bends the mind, tears the soul.

We had brought him two stones from the island, and rather shyly we handed them to him. We wondered if he would see anything in them; all we had been able to make out were the shapes of a turtle and possibly a ram. He simply glanced at them very briefly, muttered a pleased

'*Nai, nai,*' yes, – and dipped a pen into a bottle of sepia-coloured India Ink. Then, as we continued talking about the snow in Canada, the octopi we caught, the brilliant young composers in Greece who were setting some of his poems to music, his nominations for the Nobel Prize, the recent translations of his works into several languages and his own translations of the Turkish poet Nazim Hikmet, the importance of cats in one's life and the deplorable fact that some people treat their animals with more affection then they do one another, he slowly and carefully drew lines on the stones, stopping now and again to smile at his work.

'Ah, there we are,' he said finally. 'See what you think'.

On one stone he had drawn the face of what might have been a Zeus or a Poseidon with a thoughtful, gentle expression and waves of curly, bubbly hair. On the other, the angelic faces of a young man and woman gazed at one another in quiet adoration. We sat for a while in silence as the smoke from his cigarette made lyrical rings in the air, and then we took our leave, realizing with a start that it was four in the morning.

I carried the stones in a turquoise scarf, and we walked the whole way home.

The next day I wrote this poem for him – *Stones and Angels.*

> *I tried to find a stone for you to paint on, Yannis,*
> *but I found that*
> *Stones are lost sheep in golden dust*
> *Stones are the blind eyes of lost gods*
> *Stones are the stars that failed and fell here*
> *Stones are the faces of watches without hands*
>
> *Stones are the masters of time.*

And we would become masters of time, Yannis,
In the great loneliness which is God
In the mad, dynamic silence poems and icons adore.

We would paint the universe the colours of our minds
and flirt with death, but
Whether we dance or faint or kneel, we fall
On stones.

Stones are old money with which we rent the world
Forgetting that this landscape borrows us
For its own time and its own reason.

The way is open. It is paved with stones.
They are the fallen eyes of angels.

Sometimes I see Greek history in terms of a huge frieze of centaurs and humans — like the one from the temple of Zeus with its writhing, tangled group of figures fighting their way out of the stone. Great lusty bearded faces, hooves and hair and fullblown female breasts are arranged in a kind of controlled chaos as man struggles with horse-man, his powerful, inner self. In a way, Greek passion is an endless battle with the centaur — a convoluted, internal war, a war declared upon time and mortality. Penises and phalli were often stolen from ancient statues and used as fertility charms; it's almost as though history, in its wickedness, wished to castrate the mighty and mock all human endeavour.

The struggle is externalized when the centaur is an outside enemy power — and then the Greeks hurl a great NO at the face of defeat or submission. On October 28, 1940, Italy declared war on Greece, first offering the chance of a fast and painless surrender. Greece said No. *Okhi.* And that was that.

When the struggle against the Fascists ended six years later, civil war broke out, and once again the Greeks, after dealing with an outside evil, had to turn and face the evils within. History is ruthless, and nowhere more ruthless then here in *Elladha.*

It is late afternoon and the fabulous Greek light is fading. The old man who takes pictures for the tourists on the Acropolis and develops them on the spot will be packing up his tripod, his fifty year old camera and his photographic plates, and heading for home. The last slanting rays of the setting sun will lengthen his shadow on the marble stairs, and project their own dark images of the pillars of the Parthenon upon the smooth trodden stones.

'Ah, it's getting late,' says Dina, and begins to pack her knitting in a large red bag. 'Good, good,' she nods, examining my work of the last hour. 'You're improving. What is it?'

I laugh, because I'm not sure how to answer her. Then everyone laughs. The birds in their cages in the kitchen burst into crazy song, and the lemon trees in the garden quiver with some secret mirth. It is time to go.

Outside, the streets are very quiet — not like this morning, which now seems far away, when we fought our way through the crowds to reach the airline office and confirm our reservations for the flight back to Canada. It was the 28th of October, the national celebration of the day when Greece said No to the Fascist invaders. Everyone was surging downtown to see the parades. The school children in their bright blue uniforms were waving thousands of little flags; everyone was shouting and laughing, and the city was a gay pandemonium. At one point a large crowd parted down the middle like the waves of the Red Sea to allow an old general to pass. I wondered why his gait was strange, until I looked down and saw that he was walking on two wooden pegs below his knees with no crutches or support of any kind.

Later we sat in a place called, yes, The Sixth Fleet Café, and I glanced at the menu which featured strange things like Amerikan Cheese and Meet Sauce. My mind travelled back to all the places we'd been and I wasn't sure whether to laugh or cry, chuckle or scream. This is no easy country to write about; you don't really travel to it; you're either here or not here. To go among the Greeks you must be just a little mad. Mad enough to singe your wings like Icarus, to dive into the sun and fall, feathers and all, into the Aegean. You must be prepared to experience a flight of pure relentless consciousness, for something in the Greek nature demands that energy and will be constantly stretched to their limits, and that the flight be ever higher and more perilous. In this country you are drawn like a bow between heaven and earth, and you may come to know life and death as one blinding, fluid reality. The soul is the arrow shot from that bow, once only.

If then, you go among the Greeks (and you are just a little mad) — remember that everything will be demanded of you, and everything returned. Greece is a ravenous country; its hunger is a glorious, golden hunger for light, for freedom, for the pure worlds of spirit and of matter. It is a land that devours time, rushing ahead to keep a rendezvous with some unknown and miraculous destiny. It is also a land that encompasses the dark night of the soul, for the price of its kind of yearning, its kind of passion, is high. Ecstacy is never complete without the corresponding element of tragedy; if no tragedy is apparent in a situation, it often becomes necessary to invent one. The masks worn by actors in ancient Greek drama were not meant to disguise, but to *reveal* the inner man.

Greece holds up a mirror which — if we care to look — contains a reflection of the truest features of our humanity, and the predicament of our mortality. The mirror might be like the deep well in the ancient *agora* in Athens where one looks down into the darkness and almost finds oneself. Or it might be deeper and darker still, like the terrifying water reservoir at Mycenae. Or it might be clear and glittering with a thousand particles of light, like the face of the Aegean on a summer morning.

Whatever it is, it does not lie.

Greece insists that one know oneself, even if that means a lifetime of the most strenuous soul-searching, examining, questioning, and re-examining. The Greeks will not easily let things *be*, ·for existence is a multi-faceted crystal which must be turned over and over and experienced from every possible angle. Given much, they will despair that it is not enough; given nothing, they will insist that it is too much. They consume time in a desperate attempt to take hold of time. Few truths are satisfactory without corresponding half-truths to make them more palatable, more impressive. They are a people of paradox, victims of their own brilliant and contradictory awareness. Because there is no tomorrow, it is necessary to improvise it by clever intellectual manoeuvers and complicated dreams. Nothing can really be planned; only the gods make plans and very often even they botch things up terribly.

Revelling in the intensity of the moment, one despairs of the passing of the moment. Ultimately the gods are to blame for the human predicament. Man is not to blame; man is hungry, man is ambivalent, man must circle, spin, fly and dive in order to survive. There is no time, there *must be* no time to consider what it all means, because then everything would stop, and that must not happen. Suffice it to comprehend *Alpha* and *Omega*, pure worlds of spirit and of matter, and leave the letters in between to assemble their own alphabet.

As we left the Sixth Fleet Café, many people with their heads bent way back were studying the sky. A sky-writer was describing three Greek letters high above the city.

o x i — it wrote in the stark blue air. *Okhi*, which in Greek means *No* — the 'No' which was hurled at the Italian Fascists in 1940, the 'No' which sums up the attitude of Greece throughout history towards the Invader, whatever his face or his name. The 'No' which is the refusal of the Greeks to endure anything which is inhuman, demoralizing, cruel, shallow or unreal.

The word hung there and took a long, long time to vanish, first growing fuzzy the way a memory does, then breaking into particles of light.

Did I really have the ticket for home? I opened my handbag to check, and a butterfly flew out.

GWENDOLYN MacEWEN was born in Toronto in 1941. She is the author of numerous books of poetry, including *The Shadow Maker* and *Afterworlds*, which both won the Governor General's Literary Award for Poetry. She also published novels, plays, travel memoirs, and children's books. MacEwen died in 1987.

LIST

The A List

Manual for Draft-Age Immigrants to Canada Mark Satin

Passing Ceremony Helen Weinzweig

The Bush Garden Northrop Frye

Made for Happiness Jean Vanier

Hard Core Logo Nick Craine

The Big Why Michael Winter

The Little Girl Who Was Too Fond of Matches Gaetan Soucy

Death Goes Better with Coca-Cola Dave Godfrey

Basic Black with Pearls Helen Weinzweig

Ticknor Sheila Heti

This All Happened Michael Winter

Kamouraska Anne Hebert

The Circle Game Margaret Atwood

De Niro's Game Rawi Hage

Eleven Canadian Novelists Interviewed by Graeme Gibson

Like This Leo McKay Jr.

The Honeyman Festival Marian Engel

La Guerre Trilogy Roch Carrier

Selected Poems Alden Nowlan

No Pain Like This Body Harold Sonny Ladoo

Poems for all the Annettes Al Purdy

Five Legs Graeme Gibson

Selected Short Fiction of Lisa Moore

Survival Margaret Atwood

Queen Rat Lynn Crosbie

Ana Historic Daphne Mariatt

Civil Elegies Dennis Lee

The Outlander Gil Adamson

The Hockey Sweater and Other Stories Roch Carrier